Ancient Magick for
Today's Witch Series

CELTIC MAGICK

MONIQUE JOINER SIEDLAK

oshunpublications.com

Celtic Magick © Copyright 2020 Monique Joiner Siedlak

ISBN 978-1-950378-22-7 (Paperback)

ISBN 978-1-961362-22-2 (Hardback)

ISBN 978-1-950378-21-0 (eBook)

All rights reserved

The content contained within this book may not be reproduced, duplicated or transmitted without direct written permission from the author or the publisher.

Under no circumstances will any blame or legal responsibility be held against the publisher, or author, for any damages, reparation, or monetary loss due to the information contained within this book, either directly or indirectly.

Legal Notice

This book is copyright protected. It is only for personal use. You cannot amend, distribute, sell, use, quote or paraphrase any part, or the content within this book, without the consent of the author or publisher.

Disclaimer Notice

Please note the information contained within this document is for educational and entertainment purposes only. All effort has been executed to present accurate, up to date, reliable, complete information. No warranties of any kind are declared or implied. Readers acknowledge that the author is not engaged in the rendering of legal, financial, medical or professional advice. The content within this book has been derived from various sources. Please consult a licensed professional before attempting any techniques outlined in this book.

By reading this document, the reader agrees that under no circumstances is the author responsible for any losses, direct or indirect, that are incurred as a result of the use of the information contained within this document, including, but not limited to, errors, omissions, or inaccuracies.

Cover Design by MJS

Cover Images by MidJourney

Published by Oshun Publications

www.oshun_publications.com

ANCIENT MAGICK FOR TODAY'S WITCH SERIES

The *Ancient Magick for Today's Witch Series* is a series for modern witches to explore ancient magick, covering Celtic, Gypsy, and Crystal magic, among others. It offers practical advice on spells, rituals, and enchantments for today's use, incorporating natural energies and spiritual connections. With insights into Shamanism, Wicca, and more, it helps readers enhance their magickal journey, offering paths to protection, prosperity, and spiritual growth by combining ancient wisdom with contemporary practice.

Wiccan Basics

Candle Magick

Wiccan Spells

Love Spells

Abundance Spells

Herb Magick

Moon Magick

Creating Your Own Spells

Gypsy Magic

Protection Magick

Celtic Magick

Shamanic Magick

Crystal Magic

Sacred Spaces

Solitary Witchcraft

Novice Witch's Guide

MONIQUE JOINER SIEDLAK

GET UPDATES, FREEBIES & GIVEAWAYS

JOIN MY NEWSLETTER

MOJOSIEDLAK.COM/MOONLIGHT-MUSINGS

CONTENTS

Introduction	xiii
1. Introduction to the Celts	1
2. Preparing for Magic	7
3. Magical Elements	13
4. Casting the Magic Circle	17
5. Tools of Magic	25
6. The Tuatha Dé Danann	31
7. Gods and Goddesses	35
8. The Druids	47
9. Fairies and Fae Folk	53
10. The Otherworld	63
11. The Tree of Life	69
12. Celtic Festivals	75
13. Correspondences	83
14. A Few Magic Spells	91
Conclusion	97
References	99
About the Author	103
More Books by Monique	105
Don't Miss Out	109

INTRODUCTION

Most people have some interest in magic. Whether they are a teenager or adult who is looking into casting magic spells or a witch, there is a lot of information from the Druids that will help them thrive in their interests. People do not have to be interested in performing magic when it comes to learning about Celtic magic and how one can use it today.

People know very little about the Druids. Most people believe they are an ancient Celtic class that no longer exists, but many people still practice. While most Druids follow Christian teachings today, their history is varied and takes us back to around the 3rd Century BCE. You will learn all about these ancient beliefs and notice how this knowledge can help you today when it comes to casting your magic.

Chapter 1 will give you an introduction to the Celts. You will learn a bit about their history, religion, traditions, and how to understand Celtic magic.

Chapter 2 will start diving into the world of magic with its first step, which is preparing you for magic. When you ready yourself for magic, you want to think of everything possible. If you are reading a spell and you do not understand precisely what it is saying, you need to dig a little deeper. By performing a spell when you are not feeling confident, you are opening yourself up to more self-doubt and negative energy.

Chapter 3 will look at the magical elements, which are also known as the directional elements. This chapter will help you understand the four main elements of water, air, fire, and earth. You will also learn about a crucial fifth element, the spirit, that often sits at the center of your circle.

Chapter 4 discusses casting your magic circle. This is a circle of protection that you will want to form before you cast a spell. You can also place a circle of protection around yourself quickly if you feel there are any negative entities in your environment. It is essential that you cast the spell correctly and understand to keep everything closed until the spell is over. If you step out of the circle, you create a doorway that lets any entity walk in while you are performing a spell, which can be dangerous. This chapter will also discuss Esbats, the Ritual of Evocation, and the Ritual of Invocation.

Chapter 5 walks you through the necessary magical tools that you will use for Celtic magic. Most of these tools are familiar with any spellwork, but there are a couple that is considered unique to Celtic magic. This chapter will also help you set up your altar.

Chapter 6 will give you history and information on the Tuatha de Danann. This is a group of highly esteemed gods that brought special tools into Ireland and won the charge to rule most of the country. They are some of the most powerful gods in Ireland and are considered some of the oldest gods.

Chapter 7 gives you information about gods and goddesses. Not only will you learn some of the basics, but you will also get information about several specific gods and goddesses of the Celtic culture in ancient Ireland. For instance, you will learn what some of the most important gods and goddesses do and how they work. For example, if you are casting a love spell, you will know which goddess to focus on because of what she symbolizes.

Chapter 8 focuses on the Druids, some of the most influential people of the Celtic religion in Ireland. They often held occupations such as lawyers, teachers, and philosophers. However, they also had their social order, which is an integral part of history in Celtic magic. The Druids were also believed to be some of the most powerful people when it comes to magic. They taught people about magic and the Celtic way of life in special schools.

Chapter 9 takes you into the world of fairies and fae folk. Learn all about the fairies as you gain knowledge about where they live, what the Celts offered them, how they held the humans, and about a few of the specific fairies of Celtic mythology. For instance, you will read about leprechauns and the small little quiet fairies that hide in caves until they become comfortable with you, which is when they start to talk.

Chapter 10 takes you into the Celtic Otherworld, which is one of the realms in their culture where spiritual entities live. Some Celts believed that there was more than one Otherworld, while others felt there was only one. Learn how a human soul gained entry into the Otherworld after they passed away in the physical world.

Chapter 11 addresses one of the most important symbols in the Celtic world—the tree of life. What does the tree of life stand for, and why did it become so important? Why do you continue to see the tree of life today? Furthermore, this chapter will help you learn about a few of the sacred places of the Celtic world that you can still visit today and about some of their sacred animals.

Chapter 12 explains the eight main Celtic festivals of the ancient world. You will learn about how these festivals followed the seasons and their calendar. You will also gain knowledge about why the Celts celebrated each celebration as a new beginning. Learn about how some of the gods and goddesses connect to the festivals. What type of offerings and thanks they gave to the spiritual entities.

Chapter 13 is titled correspondence and gives you some necessary information that will help you with your spell casting. For instance, you will learn about incense, and how there are certain types of incense, you should use for certain spells. You will discover that each color has a specific meaning when it comes to candles and which element will have more focus, depending on what spell you are performing.

Chapter 14 is considered a bonus chapter and one that I hope helps you on your magical journey. Take a step into casting your first spell with one of the most natural spells for a beginner. You can find spells that only use herbs and some that will use your cauldron and candles.

Before you turn the page and open the door to your magical journey, I want to wish you luck. But, above all, I want you to understand that you need to always think of safety first. For instance, do not let the candle burn when you are not in the room or close by. Make sure there is nothing flammable close to the candle when it is burning. Also, always make sure that you understand the spell you are about to cast, and you fully close your circle of protection around your altar and the whole area.

1

INTRODUCTION TO THE CELTS

While no one is entirely sure when the Celts first came into existence, many looks at the 3rd Century BCE; however, some people believe they came earlier. Roman emperor Julius Caesar wrote about the Celts during his reign in the 1st Century BCE when he discussed how his military troops fought against the Celts and their belief system. Spreading throughout western Europe, the Celts lived in Ireland, France, Britain, and Spain. They migrated from land to land during their growth. During the war between the Romans and Celts, most of the Celtic groups moved into one area in Britain because the attempts to control that land by the Roman soldiers were unsuccessful. While the Celts are not as widely well-known today, they are still prominent in Britain and Ireland.

Some people believe that the Celts were barbarians, at least in their earliest centuries. This belief mainly stems from some of the earliest recorded histories during the 7th and 8th centuries when people referred to the Celts as "Galli," which means barbarians. However, they were anything but barbarians as they strove to spread their culture and beliefs across Europe.

They wanted people to learn their ways. Teaching others through their professions as teachers, judges, and priests. The Celts established their individual tribes within their population, including the Britons, Galatians, Irish, Gaels, and Gauls.

The Galatians focused their time in today's northern Spain. What is now present-day France saw mainly the Britons and Gauls. The Celtic groups spoke their own languages, such as Cornish and Welsh. Because the Celtic groups spoke so many tongues, historians believe that the Romans, Greeks, and other cultures struggled to communicate with the Celts.

The Celts were fearless people that had dozens of skills to run a civilized society. However, their primary priority was being warriors. That caused problems when it came to organizing their community as the leaders did not have the skills to organize themselves well as tribes while focusing on the warrior aspect of civilization. In fact, Celts were so well-known as fighters that they often received payment to travel to other areas and fight in wars. They had a high price tag, but this price was matched because of the strength and fearlessness the Celts possessed.

A woman in the Celtic world was treated equally to a man. It was believed that women could do nearly anything a man could do, including fighting in a war. Many women proved to be fearless and great warriors. It is rumor of the Celtic woman was that you did not want to make her angry because she had a temper, which could be dangerous, which is one reason they fought in wars.

It is good that the Celts did not fear the next battle because they often had invaders that tried to take their lands. Fortunately, the Celts won most of the battles and kept their property. However, this changed when the Romans came into Irish territory around the 1st Century BCE. Even after dozens of uprising and surprise attacks, the Celts continued to lose, and the Romans gained more control of their land. The Romans continued to hold the lands until Britain came in around 60 to 60 AD. While other countries continued to fight and win Irish territory, the beliefs that the Celts held stayed until the Christians came onto their land.

Today, most of what we know from the ancient Celts, especially the gods, goddesses, fairies, and other mythical stories, are words passed on from generation to generation. Part of this is because the Celts did not write down their history or stories until much later, as they did not like keeping written records. If anyone did write down any Celtic history, which is the case with St. Patrick, those histories were burned. One example is the approximately 180 books that St. Patrick wrote in a Celtic language.

Religion

From as far back as historians can trace the Celts, they were seen as a highly religious group of people. They followed the ethical teachings laid out for them by the Druids. These teachings were not lengthy by any means. They are summed up as follows: do not act in an evil way or engage in any evilness, be courageous and strong, honor and worship the gods and goddesses, and reincarnation does exist.

Historians get their information about Celtic religion from two main types of sources. The first is literature written by the Celts from the medieval times. The second is sculptural statues that give us clues to how they lived, dressed, and what they believed.

The Celts saw the Druids as their priesthood and followed their word, even when the Romans and other groups tried to make the Celts change their ways. To help them hold on to their religious beliefs, the Celts set up organizations of women who they called Dryads. They lived in sacred groves and were held in high spiritual esteem and compared to goddesses. Some historical writings show some of the Dryads were goddesses. For example, Elise Boulding states in her book The Underside of History that the goddess Brigid was a Dryad (Angelfire, n.d.). Some people believe that the Dryads came before the Druids, but there is no way to be sure which group came first.

Anyone in the Celtic world that was held in high religious esteem was known as a healer. Even if they hold a position such as a teacher or judge, they could heal and not just in relation to their occupation. They had special healing powers that they received from the gods to help humans on earth.

The Celts had many beliefs and practices when it came to their religion. For instance, they believed in reincarnation and that there was another world spirits went to after the physical body dies. They believed that it was up to the living to make sure the dead remained at peace and happy so that they would bury people with their favorite objects, such as ornaments and weapons. Some people were buried with food, clothing, jewelry, or anything else they enjoyed in life.

They did not believe they had to go to a specific place to worship. In fact, there is no proof that the early ancient Celts had any type of temple, but this does not mean one never existed.

By the time Christianity started spreading through Ireland during 400 AD, the Celtic traditions were set. In fact, some of the traditions began to mix in with Christianity and are still present in Ireland's culture today. For example, the shamrock, which is the country's national symbol, represents the holy spirit. The shamrock has three leaves, with one leaf representing the son, the second leaf the father, and the third leaf representing the Holy Ghost.

Sacrifice was an essential part of their culture. Public officials took part in public and private sacrifices. One of the gravest punishments was becoming barred from sacrifices. This often happened when people didn't follow through with the Druid's laws.

Understanding Celtic Magic

Magic was commonplace for the Celts as it became part of everything they did, from their thoughts to actions. They believed that magic helped people understand the world around them and defined magic as an "energetic undercurrent of the universe that is accessible from the edges of the human psyche as a force that is used to cause or create change" (Hughes, 2014).

Celtics used magic every day and didn't have any trouble reaching spiritual insight because they understood it as the world around them. They were always walking among magic, spirits, gods, and goddesses. Magic helped the spirits solidify to help the Celts in their daily lives. To the Celts, magic was a natural force and something they should not change or remove.

The Celts believed these natural forces are within everyone as they exist in the universe. The forces are a part of what you think, feel, believe, say, and do. Magic connects the worlds and everything around it. Take a moment to think of a spider's web how each line of the web connects to form a home for the spider. The web connects the spider's world to our world because we can see and feel it. Other insects and objects can get trapped in the spider's world, where the spider can decide to set anything free. Of course, we can also destroy the spider's web with a single touch.

The Celtic world and belief in magic are different from our modern-day beliefs. Today, some people struggle with the thoughts of magic or believing in magic. People don't want to believe in the witch law that the Celts followed throughout their lives. For centuries, people have entreated the modern mind to believe that the magic the Celts used is bad or evil. People have taught that magic, witch laws, and witches are a fantasy and not of this world. Therefore, many people fear the thoughts of witches, their laws, and magic coexisting in our world. The Celts did not fear any part of magic or their laws. They felt that other people should follow these ways because magic helps guide a person throughout their life.

People tend to believe that Druidcraft and Wicca are the same, but they are two different spiritual paths. However, they do have a lot of similarities. Like Wicca, Druidcraft is a way of freedom and empowerment. They draw their inspiration from ancient practices but continuously work on evolving their practices as well. Druidcraft does not expect people to follow strict guidelines when practicing magic. Instead, the craft gives you inspiration from the past and allows you to find your unique path. In a way, the same way the Druids practice religion is the same way they practice Druidcraft. Your search for the answers to your spirituality and craft inside of you. Druidcraft does not offer all the "right" answers because you need to search for the answers that fit you.

To truly understand Celtic magic, you have to realize that at the end of the day, there is you and the sky. There is the ocean and you. There is the land and you. It is only you and what is around you.

2

PREPARING FOR MAGIC

No matter what type of magic you perform, you always need to make sure you understand the steps thoroughly. You need to have a grasp on what you believe, feel, what you want, need, the goal you have in mind, and the concepts of the magic. You need to learn as much as possible before you even begin to cast your magical circle and perform a spell.

The biggest reason for understanding all the factors associated with magic will focus on your beliefs. Still, most people believe it is best always to know precisely what you want and what you are doing, so you do not let any negative energy into your magic. For example, many Wiccans and witches believe that if they do not close their magical circle correctly after performing their spell, negative entities, such as demons, can enter through a portal and stop the spell from working. Other people believe that these negative entities can continue to harm them or the people they love. Therefore, they make sure they know how to close their magic circle correctly, so only the peaceful and positive energies they called to help them cast the spell are in their presence.

Preparation for any kind of magic requires knowledge and self-discipline. You need to learn about several techniques, such as concentration, meditation, and visualization.

Self-discipline is when you learn to control your feelings by overcoming your weaknesses. This does not mean that you stop feeling or work on ignoring your emotions. You want to do the exact opposite of ignoring—you want to pay attention to the way you feel and work through the emotion. For example, you are reading the latest headlines on Facebook and come across someone in your area that is accused of animal abuse. Immediately, you become angry and think about what you will say the next time you see this criminal in the grocery store. When you strengthen your self-discipline, you want to acknowledge the way you feel and your thoughts, but you work through the feelings and thoughts, so you do not react negatively. You gain control over your actions by controlling your emotions. Look at it this way—you respond in specific ways because of the way you feel. If you are sad, you will cry, and if you are happy, you will smile. Therefore, if you work through your anger towards the criminal, you are less likely to react in a negative way when you meet the person in the grocery store.

Self-discipline is an area in your life that you always need to work on. Fortunately, there are dozens of techniques you can use to improve, such as learning your weaknesses, removing temptations, and forgiving others so you can move forward. If you know you lack self-discipline, you will want to improve this area of yourself before you start focusing on the techniques necessary for magic preparation. Once you have a strong sense of how to control your emotions, you can move on to increase your concentration, visualization, and meditation.

When you hold an idea or image in your mind for a period of time without interruption, you are concentrating. The main reason you want to increase your concentration for magic is that you need to exclude outside noise and thoughts. You need to focus directly on what you are doing for the magic to give you the best results. For example, if you live in a busy city, you need to block outside interference, such as car horns.

Exercises You Can Do

There are two main exercises that you can follow to increase your concentration. For the first exercise, you can use an image. You want to make sure that you are happy with the picture. For example, if you Google pictures of candles and you are drawn to an image of a purple candle with the shape of a heart around it, you will use this image. You can also find a picture from your home, phone, or even a card from your tarot deck. Once you have chosen your image, hang the picture, or stand it up against an object. You want the image at a comfortable level as you will concentrate on it for some time. This means if you aren't comfortable standing for several minutes, you want to sit down. After looking at the picture for a period of time, close your eyes and try to imagine every detail with your mind's eye. Continue to keep that image in your mind for as long as possible.

The second exercise involves a lit candle. You can use any candle, but you want to place it on a safe location, such as a table. Sit in a comfortable position and focus your attention on the flame of the candle. You should stare at the bottom or the blue part of the flame, as this is less strainful for your eyes. If you find that you cannot concentrate on the flame because it hurts your eyes, blow out the candle, and follow the first exercise. Always remember to blink when you need to. This is not a staring contest, and you always want to ensure that you are putting the health of your eyes and body above the exercise. After several minutes, close your eyes and continue to imagine the flame. You do not need to imagine the candle, just the flame. Hold the image in your mind's eye for as long as possible.

You can practice these exercises as much as you want to. You can set a stopwatch and time yourself on how long the activity takes. Record your numbers as you will find yourself concentrating on the object and image in your mind's eye for a more extended period over time.

Meditation

Like concentration, meditation is a technique that can help you in all areas of your life. It is best to meditate in the morning for 10 to 15 minutes. You want to find a location where you will not be interrupted and can focus. This can be a challenge for some people, especially if you have younger children. One of the best tips many busy parents give is that you need to get up about a half-hour before your children usually get up. This allows you plenty of time to wake yourself up and get your meditation time before your children start to wake up.

There is no right or wrong way to meditate, but it is best to start in a quiet room so you can remain focused. However, if soothing music helps you focus, then you will want to play it lightly while you meditate. Make sure all your distractions are off, such as your cell phone and television.

Find a comfortable place to lay or sit down. Start to relax your body by taking a few deep and slow breaths. Once you feel your muscles relax, imagine a white light surrounding your body. This is your light of protection that follows you wherever your imagination takes you.

Imagine yourself walking toward a body of water. This water can be a peaceful waterfall, or it can be water running under a bridge. Stand beside the water or on the bridge and imagine yourself dropping all of your problems into the water. You might hear a splash as they hit the water or see ripples. Once you have dumped all of your problems, walk away from the water.

Now, take yourself to a peaceful location. You might find yourself on a farm full of animals and wildflowers or in a meadow. Walk around your peaceful area and take in as much of the calm and healing nature possible. Talk to your spirit guides or the spirits within nature as they will start to help guide you through your magical world.

Once you start to meditate, you will begin to open up your mind to your spirit guides, gods, goddesses, or any power you believe in. It is in your peaceful meadow that you will start to hear them talk to you. Listen carefully as they might sound like the wind. They will help guide you to an answer to all the problems you previously dropped in the water.

A word of caution is that you always need to ensure that you have the white light around you. Because meditation brings you into an astral state, you might find entities that are not welcoming. You could see them, or you might simply feel afraid or uncomfortable. When this happens, you need to focus on your white light of protection and leave the area.

You can leave your meditative state at any time. All you need to do is focus on your body. For example, notice how your clothing feels on your skin when you breathe. Once you are aware of your body, open your eyes, and continue your morning.

Meditation will also help you with your concentration and visualization. Concentration strengthens through meditation because you need to focus on your breath, body, and your mind. Visualization increases because you imagine a series of events.

Visualization also becomes stronger when you focus on what you want to achieve. You have goals that you want to reach throughout your life. It does not matter if they are long-term or short-term goals. You want to visualize the steps it takes to achieve these goals and celebrate your achievements.

You want to be as detailed as possible when you visualize. Take your time to write down the steps you will take to reach your goal before you start visualizing. Focus on one step at a time by treating each step as its own mini-goal.

Your Self Image

Another factor to consider when you are preparing is your confidence. If you suffer from low self-esteem or self-confidence, you want to build up your confidence. You can use meditation to help you along this path by visualizing yourself, casting the magic successfully. You want to follow all the steps laid out with the spell, as this will boost your confidence without needing to perform the spell.

Another form of preparing for magic is by learning the ritual magic or spells that you want to focus on. You might have an idea in mind, such as love or money spell, and prepare by reading more information about these spells. You want to find the perfect spell for you, your goals, and what you believe.

Many people like to think about a time and a day that is best for casting magic. For example, you might look at the phases of the moon or certain holidays. Make time for your magic by keeping your schedule clear during that time.

3

MAGICAL ELEMENTS

All magic will contain at least one of the four natural elements: water, fire, earth, and air. Ancient Druids believed that everyone is made up of these four elements. These elements are connected to the four directions (North, East, South, and West). They are made up of the universe and everything around us. The ingredients that make up the four elements have been around since the beginning, which is one reason why we cannot exist without them.

While the four elements work together, they are also independent. They each have their own positive and negative traits. Each element have their own magical purposes, qualities, and personalities. For the Celts, there are colors associated with the four elements. These are a bit different from the ceremonial magic of today. For the ancient Celts, the colors were red for the east, grey for the west, white for the south, and black for the north. To further explain the colors, the Celts believed that red was the rising of the sun, white was the middle of the day, twilight was grey, and midnight was black.

Fire

Fire was the essential element to the Celts. When you cast your magic circle, fire manages the south part and is considered to be a dry and warm element, which is why it is connected to the sun. When thinking of fire, think of an "aha" moment, as it is this element that causes you to act on your thinking and sometimes impulses. Fire's ruler is Djin, and it looks over the sunbeams. When it comes to fire's positive characteristics, you want to think about a warm day at the beach. Fire is a lover of freedom and a dreamer. People who associate themselves with fire show willpower, leadership, enthusiasm, and courage. It associates with summer, candles, the sun, blood, and a dagger and sword. The negative characteristics are fear, an inflated ego, conflicts, hate, a devastating fire, war, anger, and jealousy. On the psychological level, your element of fire shows when you are creating or feel "fired up." When your psychological level is too high, you will start to feel the negative characteristics, but when you are at a healthy level, you will feel the positive traits (Louv, 2018).

Air

Air manages the eastern part of the circles and is ruled by Paralda, who supervises the spirits and fairies of nature, Sylphs, and Zephyrs. Like fire, the air is considered warm but is also moist. It associates with spring, sunrise, clouds, a breeze, joy, optimism, breath, cognitive quickness, and helpfulness. It is the element that is logical in nature and helps you with complex issues. Think of the problems a scientist or mathematician will create and solve and associate this with air. Therefore, this is the element you want to focus on when you have an incredibly complex problem that is intellectual. Negatively, it associates with forgetfulness, storms that involve wind like hurricanes and tornadoes, gossip, inability to focus, and any type of destruction that requires wind.

Earth

The Earth governs the northern part of the circle. Its ruler is Ghom, who manages the moonbeams, dwarfs, and gnomes. This element gives off a dry and cool feel with positive associations like ritual salt, caves, mountains, the pentacle, responsibility, understanding, and believing in life's purpose, winter, midnight, soil, respect, and stability. Negatively, it is associated with an inability or lack of willingness to change, stubbornness, earthquakes, mudslides, not willing to see or understand the problem, and lack of conscience. Earth is our manifestation in the physical world. You always need the other three elements when it comes to achieving earth, and with the right amount of each element, you will be able to bring anything into the physical world.

Water

Water oversees the western part of the circle and is ruled by Niksa. This ruler looks after the little ones of the lakes, springs, rivers, and ponds. It's associated with a moist and cool place and has positive associations like fall, sunset, peacefulness, helpfulness, love, forgiveness, compassion, and intuition. The negative associations are rainstorms or anything that is destroyed by water, floods, and inability to control your emotions, laziness, and insecurity. When you feel inspired, you are feeling water. This inspiration often comes from the universe, artists, and other places. Water is stronger for some people because they think more deeply than other people. For instance, an empath is a person who is known to feel someone else's emotions. They internalize this emotion so much that they can start to feel the same physical pain that the other person feels. It is important to pay attention to your instincts, emotions, and inspirations because they will help you find the answers to the problems you dropped in the water. You might find the answers when you are reading a book, watching a movie, looking at a random sign in the subway, or in your dreams. Sometimes these answers can pop out at you in your thoughts and emotions (Louv, 2018).

When it comes to the Druids, there are not only the four main directional elements but also a fifth element—spirit. This element is considered to manage the center of the circle. Therefore, it helps the other four elements create a balance among themselves. The spirit also looks at the gods and goddesses. Many Druids considered the spirit as the most crucial entity as it is the final piece of the puzzle for making your desires real.

4

CASTING THE MAGIC CIRCLE

First, you need to understand what casting the magic circle means. Think of it like an office where you work. On the first day, you bring pictures of your family, books, pens, pencils, and anything else you need to set up your desk for work. You set up your office so you can ensure you have everything you need to get your task done. The same goes with a magic circle. You create a temporary space where you can perform your ritual or magic. Your magic circle can move from place to place, or you can set up an altar and keep your circle in one location.

A magic circle is not imaginary if done correctly. The energies of the circle will allow you to feel the circle. If you are clairvoyant or hold other spiritual powers, you can see the circle as long as you are in tune with your senses.

The circle is seen as magical because it does not have a beginning or an end. Therefore, it is often considered a symbol of eternity, which is precisely what the Celts thought of a circle. Think of the circle as the foundation of your magic. Your five elements will sit within the circle, you are protected, and all your magic happens within the circle. You can compare the circle to the sacred drawing of your magic.

It is essential to make sure you draw the circle with a sword or dagger. The main reason why is because this gives you more protection and helps keep any negative entities away from your magic. If any type of negativity, including bad thoughts, gets in the way of your magic, it will not work as it should. If the negative forces are bad enough, the result will become the opposite of what you hope.

Another reason you draw the circle in a certain way is that it helps raise the power within the circle. People can see the power that arises in the circle as it makes a cone with the circle as its base. Many people believe that it is this powerful cone that caused people to associate witches with pointed hats.

For the Celts, another vital piece of the magic circle is the wheel-cross. Similar to a Christian cross, it is surrounded by a circle. It is important to ensure that you have a wheel-cross for your magic because this cross will not only aid in protection, but it will also give you a balance of entities and forces. For instance, it balances the female and male energies along with the four directional elements and the fifth spiritual element.

Typically, a magic circle is about nine to ten feet in circumference. You will place candles to represent the five elements. Sometimes people also have certain symbols to represent the elements as well.

Before you start casting your circle, you want to make sure that all the supplies you will need are right there. Casting the magic circle means that you seal it from any negative energy that is outside of the circle. You can break the barrier and let this negative energy inside if you step outside of the circle. You should never step outside of the circle until the ritual is complete, and you have thanked all of the elements, gods, goddesses, and other spirits that helped you perform the magic.

Ritual of Evocation

The ritual of evocation has been a Celtic practice since ancient times. Today, there are several ways that you can perform this ritual, just as there seem to be a few different ways the ancient Celts performed it. The point of a ritual of evocation is to call upon spirits, gods, goddesses, or other supernatural entities. Celts believed that the entities they called upon during the ceremony helped them with their magic. People still follow this belief because it is the spiritual entities that help give you the spell that you are casting. They will not only help you through the process of casting but also help heal and assist you with anything you need and ask from them.

Some people will perform the ritual of evocation with several tools. For example, you will need three white, unscented candles, the five elements represented by oils, dressing cloth for the candles, a knife to carve the candles, a lighter, candle holders, and a candle snuffer. You can also include a sword, wand, chalk if you want a visualization of the circle, paper, and a writing utensil to write down any information, and any incense that will help raise the energy of the environment.

Other people will perform this ritual more straightforwardly, with five candles and a sword. They will draw the circle and then set the candles in the designated spots. Most people like to start with the east candle, which is the candle of water. With each candle, you want to make sure that you connect with them in some way. You might do this by touching them and saying, "I give this candle the element of water, taken from my body and soul," and moving your hand in a clockwise motion around the candle. This allows your energies to connect with the candle's energies.

Rituals of Invocation

The ritual of invocation is similar to evocation in the fact that you are calling spiritual entities to help you with your magic. However, with evocation, you call on them, and they assist you while outside of your body. Invocation is requesting the assistance of the entities to help you with the ritual through your soul and body. Think of invocation as an invitation for the entity.

With invocation, you want to call forth a particular spirit or deity because of their powers and characteristics. You know this distinct entity can help you because of the powers they possess.

One of the key factors about an invocation is that you have to say it out loud. You need to call forth the spirit using your words and not your thoughts. Speaking overthinking is always important when you are performing magic because there are a lot of magical properties that come from the sound of your words and your breath. Your five senses are always an essential part of the magic and should never be ignored.

The ritual of invocation can become more dangerous than evocation because you often request that the spirit enter your body. This means that they take possession of you, such as in channeling and mediumship. The danger comes if you do not cast a circle of protection around yourself correctly or if you break the boundary. If this happens, you can easily let in a negative entity instead of the spirit that you requested. While this is known to be a rare occurrence, it can and has happened.

The Esbats

The Esbat is known as the full moon, a special time during the month when most Celts perform their magic. No matter what type of magic or witchcraft people cast, they will often focus on it during the full moon because the energies from the moon are more powerful. If you want to perform a ritual of invocation, Celts believe this is the best time for you to do so. Many Esbat celebrations will have a ritual of invocation. The ancient ritual for this time was known as Drawing Down the Moon. The ritual was usually completed as the main event of the celebration and focused on the Mother Goddess spirit that represented the full moon.

In the ancient days, the Celtic year was divided into 13 months by following the full moons. Each month had one full moon. For the Celts, each moon had a name, gender, and nicknames. For instance, the Ash moon was feminine, and her nickname was the Moon of Waters. Many moons had more than one nickname, such as the Ivy Moon, who was masculine and given the nicknames "Moon of Resilience" and Moon of Buoyancy" (McCoy, 1995).

To cast a circle, you will want to make sure all of your magical tools are near your altar. One of the first steps you will take is lighting any incense that you plan on using as the scents will help prepare the scene and will open your subconscious mind, which is essential when you are casting magic. You can keep the incense burning, but remember to think of safety first. You want to have some type of holder for your incense, so it does not start to burn any object.

Set your specific candles on their designated places. For example, you might set the red candle on the east and the white on the south. This will further help you create an environment where your magic can thrive. Of course, you will want to use a form of light in your magic space, so you can see what is going on. You can do this by safely lighting candles around your area or turn on a lamp. Make sure you are dressed for casting magic, such as a robe or cloak.

Set your altar along with all other supplies between all the candles. Most people will face east as this is the direction in which the sun rises, which means it is the beginning of a new day. To help create a mood or strengthen the environment you want, you can play specific music, such as relaxation or meditation music.

Using your dagger, start with the east and visualize a protective white or blue shield around you. Imagine this protective shield growing from you to beyond the candles. Aim the tip of the dagger's blade to the floor and move clockwise from the east to create a circle. Make sure that you completely close the circle, meaning that ends at the east overlap. If you do not have a dagger or a sword, you can use your finger to draw the circle. The most important part of drawing the circle is that you say the following or similar words (there are many variations, and you can also make up your own wording that shows why you are casting the circle and what you want from the higher powers):

"With this circle, I concentrate on the power of the ancient gods. I ask that they help me and bless me as I am their child. I stand here between two worlds and ask for the ancient gods and goddesses (**you can say specific names**) to come and help me. I ask that they protect me as they walk me through this magical journey."

Once your circle is set, you can start your spell. The most important factor is you do not break the circle as this can let in negative entities. You should also remember that if you feel threatened over the following weeks after performing the spell, you can redo the circle, and it will protect you again. All you need to do is visualize surrounding yourself with the protective circle.

5

TOOLS OF MAGIC

Magic is one of those topics that is a little tough to explain, but people believe it works. Some people use magic as often as possible and became great leaders, while other people focus on magic when they need to. Of course, there are still many skeptics in the world, but this does not take away from your magic.

When you are casting magic, you will use specific objects or tools of magic, words, and movements that will send messages to your higher power, nature, and Mother Earth, letting them know what needs to be done. If the magic is performed correctly, what you need or something extraordinary will happen.

Many factors determine the success of your magic. One of these factors I have touched on before and this is making sure that your circle is closed. There is no way for any negativity to get into your circle. When negativity is allowed in, you will find that the spell does not work well or at all. The opposite that you ask for can happen. This negativity is not only spirits or entities; it also refers to your thoughts and emotions. It relates to your belief that the spell will work, and all will be well. There is also the self-discipline factor. It is understanding that you have to concentrate on the task at hand for the spell to work well. If you only perform magic with half your belief, heart, and thoughts, you will not get results.

When you perform your magic, you will want to ensure that you go back to Chapter 2, so you are well prepared. You will also want to go back to Chapter 4 to ensure you cast your circle correctly. In Chapter 13, you will get a lot of information about what candles and incense to use in your spells. You will also know which element will help you with what spell. All of these chapters will work together to give you the best outcome for your magic.

For Celtic magic, there are several basic tools that you will use. Some of these tools are an altar, pentacle, cauldron, wand, armband, incense, incense burner, herbs, sword, knife, headband, staff, goblets, robes, and stones.

The first step you will want to take is to make sure you have a special location for your magic. This is sometimes easier if you live alone or with other people who are open to your wishes (we all know, not everyone is). While it is ideal to have a special room set up for your magic, it is the case for many people that they can only have part of a room. Your altar does not have to be big; it can be as small as a coffee table or as large as a room. You might choose to set up your altar in your bedroom and use the top of your desk or dresser. There are specific tables that you can buy for your magic, but they are not necessary but are available to purchase. For example, you might find a small chest with one drawer, which will allow you to keep some of your supplies.

You can decorate your altar any way you wish. There is no right or wrong way to do this, and it is usually a matter of personal preference. You might find scarves to drape across your altar, where you place a couple of candles. You might also have a little cauldron, herbs, and symbols sitting on the top. It is all up to you. The key is to make it your space. You want to create a space that is not only magical but peaceful. A place where you feel comfortable and relaxed—free of negative thoughts or emotions.

Symbols of the elements are one of the many items that people use to decorate their altar. For example, having a bowl of sand to represent the north and incense to represent the east. There are different symbols that you can use for each direction so that you can adapt the symbol to the amount of space for your altar. These are a book of spells, wand, spirit candle (also the fifth element), paper, writing utensils, and a bowl to place any of your thoughts or notes.

A cauldron represents the element of water, which means you will need to have this for your magic. You do not need to purchase a big cauldron as a small kettle with a bail handle will work. You will usually fill the cauldron with water before you start the magic, and sometimes you will sprinkle herbs in the cauldron.

Your wand and staff should be wood, and you want to make sure that they hold your emotions and vibrations. You can purchase them at a store or have them made. Either way, once you receive these items, you want to spend time with them. Hold them without performing a spell and let the wand or staff get to know you and understand where your energies are coming from. You do not need to find a long wand. Many people state it should only be the size of your forearm or smaller. The staff will work the best if it goes up to your shoulder. Do not worry if you like a wand that has a stone, crystal, or symbol on the end of it. If you feel drawn to the wand, you need to get it. There is always a reason you feel drawn to an object, whether you are looking for it at the time or not.

One of the most personal pieces on your altar is the armband and headband. Men usually wear gold, while women wear silver. The moon can be found on the headband for the woman, and the man's headband has the symbol of the sun.

The goblet you use can be any size. The key is that it is big enough to hold water. You do not need to fill your goblet with water like you do your cauldron as your goblet will sometimes remain empty during the spellwork.

While you might want to find a dagger or sword that is older, it is best if it is new. If you decide to use a knife, you want this to be new as well. The size you choose will depend on what you feel is best when you are looking for the item. The best length for the sword is between 17 to 25 inches, but they can be a bit smaller or bigger. The most important part about the sword is you can handle it, meaning it is not too heavy. You might not find yourself using the sword often, as spells usually call for a dagger, but if you cannot handle the sword, something terrible can happen, and this can negatively affect your outcome.

When you look for candles, crystals, stones, and herbs, you want to think about what type of collection you want. Each color, whether it is on a candle, stone, or incense, works for certain spells. For example, love spells will often call for a pink candle.

One factor in realizing when it comes to your spellwork is that you will grow as you learn. For instance, you might not use tarot cards now, but you will find yourself using them down the road. Do not push yourself to learn faster than you should. It is okay to learn at a slow pace when you are working with magic. Slow is always the best place because you are less likely to make mistakes and will feel more comfortable as you grow in your magic. You might find yourself buying more tools than you place on your altar right away. This is fine. You can start with four candles and work your way up. You might find that you start with candles and then include herbs and incense at a later date. No matter what you do, the key is to always go at a slow and steady pace. This is the best speed when it comes to growing with your magic.

6
THE TUATHA DÉ DANANN

The Tuatha Dé Danann are what the children of the goddess Danu are called. It is believed that these children are the reincarnations of several people who were forced to leave Ireland for various reasons. They went and settled in northern Europe, promising to come back one day and control the land. They had a vision for Ireland and came from places such as the sky and islands far away from Ireland. Many Celts believed that they came from four main cities: Falia, Goria, Findias, and Murias. The myth of the Tuatha states that these four cities taught the gods everything they needed to know from their magic to art skills.

Between them, the Tuatha Dé Danann had many skills, but they were all skilled in magic and poetry. Other skills that became popular among the tribe were war, art, and craft skills. They were known to excel in many subjects, which they learned after they were forced to leave. Some of these subjects included civilization and science. The children received these skills through the treasures they brought with them. They were always seen with these treasures and took great pride and care in them. Without the riches, the Tuatha Dé Danann would not have had the magic to help and protect people.

Nuada is one of the children and the king of the Tuatha Dé Danann. He is the god of healing, warfare, and the sea. He brought with him, from the city of Findias, the great sword of light, or the invincible sword. The story goes, the wizard and poet of Findias, Uiscias, crafted the sword specifically for Nuada. The sword held magical powers that would not release anyone once it was drawn for them. In writing, Celts described it as a glowing white sword, similar to a torch. While it looked like a sword, it had a light that people had never seen in any sword before, which is why they believed it held magical powers.

Nuada held the title as king before the gods and goddesses came to Ireland. When they arrived, Nuada challenged Fir Bolg to a battle, which is now known as the First Battle of Mag Tuired, when he could not gain half of the land through bargaining. The Tuatha Dé Danann won the battle and allowed control of some of the land (The Celtic Journey, 2013).

Lugh is the god of light, craft, and sun. He is also known as the master of skills and one of the most powerful gods. He received his spear of victory from the city of Gorias from Esras. The most famous story that includes the spear comes from the second battle when Lugh used his weapon to kill his grandfather. At first, people did not believe that the spear held magical powers like the sword, which meant that Lugh could never rule the land. However, once Lugh killed with his spear, he proved he would make an excellent ruler as the spear held similar characteristics to the sword of light.

The Celtic god Dagda is the influential leader of the Tuatha Dé Danann. He received his cauldron from the city of Murias from a man named Semias. It is this gift that people know very little about but does realize it possessed some sort of magic as all of the four gifts did. One story states that the cauldron could bring people back from the dead.

The last gift the children brought with them was the Stone of Destiny, also known as the Stone of Fal or Lia Fail, from the city of Falias. The myth of this stone states that if the right king of Ireland places his foot against the stone, it will cry out. Many people believe you can still see this stone today if you visit the Hill of Tara.

Some people did not call the Tuatha Dé Danann gods or goddesses because they were something a bit different—entities more powerful than most gods and goddesses. They also were not considered fairies. Instead, some Celts felt they were a rare Druidic race that worked closely with nature. They were a group of scientific people who understood how to operate the laws of nature more thoroughly than anyone else, which gave them a special knowledge that many people saw as a magical power.

The question of who the Danann truly were comes because of their physical characteristics. At the time, native people of Ireland were known as short, tiny, and having dark skin. However, the Danann is described as having blonde or red hair, taller than any human, and having green or blue eyes. They were also seen with pale skin, which gave them a lighter and more holy appearance to the Celts.

The Myth of the Tuatha Dé Danann

The legend of the Tuatha Dé Danann talks about how they came from a mist from the water. The proof of how they got to the coastline is all but lost. However, many Celts assumed that they burned their boats, as this gave them the best chance of not leaving the land again.

When they landed, the ruler of Ireland was Eochid, the son of Erc. He was not impressed by the Danann, especially when they came to him to negotiate some of the lands. This is how the first battle erupted, giving most of the land to the Danann. The main reason why they did not take all the land is that they wanted to respect Eochid and the Fir Bolg, which is what the people of Ireland called themselves.

While many people did not know what to expect from their new rulers, they were anything but afraid. The Danann proved to be respectful and civilized people who truly cared about the people on their land. They were happy to introduce their skills to the Fir Bolg, who soon held the rulers in high regard.

Because Nuada lost his arm in the battle, he could no longer run the country as king. Therefore, Breas became king, but the people threw him out several years later because of the way he ruled. They then requested that Nuada became king once again. He accepted this position and had a new arm made of silver so he could justly rule.

A second victory came when Breas returned with a trained army. Like the first battle, the Danann proved to be stronger than Breas and his army. But, the battle would see the death of King Nuada. In his place, his brother Lugh became Ireland's new king (Ireland-information.com, n.d.).

7
GODS AND GODDESSES

Everyone has their own beliefs. For example, Christians have a dualistic view as they believe in God and the Devil. Both of these spirits are powerful and influence a person and how they act. Other religions and ethnicities do not have a dualistic view. However, most people still hold on to the belief that there is some type of higher power, like a spiritual entity that guides them throughout their day. For example, some people, like the Druids, believe in gods and goddesses.

Druids do not believe that there is one higher power. They do not have a sense of divinity that is external to the world. Druids believe that matter and spirit combine and bring a sacred union into the world. Once a person realizes this union, it continues to live in their daily lives and helps them follow the Druidry path.

There are several gods and goddesses that the Celts called forth to help them in their daily lives, with special events, and in their magic.

Aengus

Aengus, also written as Angus or Aonghus, is the god of youth, love, and poetic inspiration. He comes from Dagda and Boann and is one of the Tuatha Dé Danann. One of his most exciting facts is that he was conceived and born on the same day. He holds a gold harp that plays music, which the birds turn into love songs and messages. When the Celts offer him food, they choose strawberries, or they place his favorite flower, the red rose, in place of food. Aengus shows in several animal forms, such as the deer, dove, sparrow, and cat.

Aine

Aine is the goddess of love and fertility. She is connected to wealth, fertility, luck, earth, magic, nature, sovereignty, the sun, and summer. With her powers, Aine controls the animals and crops and is often tied to agriculture, especially when the Celts had good yields. However, her strongest association is with the animals and livestock, who she spends her time protecting. She is a Tuatha Dé Danann, where she is referred to as the Queen of the Fae. The Celts believed she would have relationships with human males and become pregnant with their child, giving birth to the first magical humans.

She is associated with many animals that she can transform into when seen, such as cows, swans, horses, birds, and rabbits. She is associated with several crystals when it comes to casting magic, including the pearl, garnet, moonstone, and quartz. Her element is fire or earth, and when Celts gave her an offering, they gave her fire. She mainly comes out from the Otherworld during midsummer.

Ana

Ana is also known as the goddess Danu or Dana. She is most commonly known as the goddess of water but is also connected to magic, rivers, wisdom, fertility, nurturing of the land, cultivation, abundance, prosperity, and wells She is Tuatha Dé Danann's mother goddess, who is sometimes seen as a god. Her most common animal forms are seagulls, snakes, mares, and salmon. She is the element of water and earth and comes around during the Imbolc festival. When the Celts gave her offerings, they laid out apples, cauldrons of water, keys, and blossoms.

Belenus

Belenus is sometimes written as Beli Mawr, Belenos, Bel, and Belenos. He is the sun god, as his name means the shining god. He is commonly believed to have pastoral characteristics as he holds healing powers from the sun and is connected to purification. He is also connected to fire as the sun god. Other connections he holds are crops, prosperity, science, success, vegetation, and fertility. When seen, he is riding in his chariot across the sky and can often be seen moving the sun with him. Other drawings show him riding lightning bolts and carrying a wheel, which he uses a shield.

Brigid

Brigid is spelled in several ways, such as Brighid, Brighit, and Brigit. However, no matter what version you see, she is known as the Hearth Goddess of Ireland, whose name means the "exalted one." As the daughter of Dagda, she is one of the Tuatha Dé Dannan, along with her two sisters, who go by the same name. The Celts often saw the sisters as a single goddess but with three characteristics, which made her unique in comparison to other goddesses.

Brigid is considered a goddess of fertility, fire, hearth, crafts, martial arts, and all-female arts. She is known as a protector, healer, magician, and a patron of the poets. She held a lot of knowledge when it came to magic, primarily if it focused on animals, love, agriculture, learning, and inspiration.

Brigid could show up in many forms, such as a warlike figure and many animals. The women believed she watched over them as they gave birth and would continue to visit their newborn baby, at least during the first couple of weeks. Because of this, many pregnant women and mothers of newborns honored her in their home.

Cailleach

Cailleach is the goddess of winter, often bringing the storms. She is the ruler of darkness who is also known as a creator and a harvest goddess. She shows up in late fall, which is around the time the Celts believed the earth was dying as everything turned brown and leaves fell off the trees. Celts portrayed her as a woman with bad teeth and one eye. Her hair was matted, and she sometimes wears a veil. Her name means old woman, but to many, she was seen as a hero who would be kind and gentle when people treated her in this manner. However, if you were cruel to her, she would bring one of her nasty storms to teach you a lesson.

Camulos

Camulos is the god of war who was associated with Mars. His symbol is the boar, and he often held a sword which had swung with great might. Many Celts depicted him with ram-like horns.

Cernunnos

Cernunnos is a god with horns that is associated with the forest. He symbolizes masculine energy, fertility, love in the physical world, woodlands, crossroads, warriors, wealth, reincarnation, and animals. Cernunnos is referred to as the god of all wild things and nature.

Cerridwen

Cerridwen is also written as Ceridwen and Caridwen. She is the goddess of nature and connected to regeneration, magic, herbs, knowledge, astrology, poetry, spells, fertility, inspiration, and death. Celts called her the keeper of the cauldron because of her magical knowledge and often called on her to help with spells. Because of this, her symbol is a cauldron.

Dagda

Dagda is known as the father god of Ireland and is often depicted as a father figure. He is also known as the god of the earth and considered the leader of the Tuatha Dé Danann. Dagda has an important role in helping create Irish stories, especially of invasions. He is associated with a cauldron, magic harp, and magic club.

Diancecht

Diancecht is the god of medicine and healing. He is known as one of the strongest healers for the Tuatha Dé Danann. The only wound that Diancecht could not heal was decapitation. However, one Celtic mythical story states that he was able to mend the arm of King Nuada by giving him a silver arm.

Epona

Epona is the goddess of fertility. She is also associated with dogs, crops, prosperity, healing springs, and maternity. She is strongly connected to the horse and seen as their protector and breeder. She is often compared to Rhiannon as they have some of the same characteristics. For example, both are connected to horses and seen as a companion to the dead. However, one of the most significant differences between the two is Epona is a goddess, whereas Rhiannon is seen as a queen.

Eriu

Eriu is the matron goddess of Ireland. With her two sisters, Banba and Fodla, she forms a trinity of goddesses. She is one of the Tuatha Dé Danann's queens and is the element of earth when called upon to help with magic.

Ernmas

Ernmas is a mother goddess who is associated with the Tuatha Dé Danann. She is the mother of Banba, Erui, and Fodla, who create a trinity of goddesses. She is also the mother of a trinity of gods as her sons are Coscar, Gnim, and Glonn. During the first battle of Mag Tuired, Ernmas was killed.

Flidais

Flidais is the goddess of the woodlands, forests, and wild things. She is known as a shape-shifter, so she can quickly change shape. She usually transforms herself into animals, which are often seen as the beasts in the forest because she is the ruler of wild beasts. When the Celts saw her, they saw her riding in a chariot that was pulled by a deer. They also saw how she had beautiful long hair, which is one of her signature features.

One story about Flidais goes that she had a herd of cattle and could receive magical milk from them because they were magical cows. She would often milk these cows and bring the milk to the physical world as it helped people stay healthy and heal. During the wars, Flidais would bring magical milk to the soldiers as it not only gave them strength but also kept them safe.

Grannus

Grannus is a god of healing springs and is also known as a sun god. When the ancient Celts worshipped Grannus, they did so along with Sirona next to him. He is connected to the element of water and identified with Apollo.

Great Father

Great Father was a god that most Celts, no matter where they lived, believed in. He was a horned god and known as the Lord. He oversaw the harvest, the sky, land of the dead, powers of destruction, lust, animals, powers of regeneration, and was the male principle of creation and mountains. Many felt that he was also the Lord of the winter and sometimes called him by this name in prayer.

Great Mother

Great Mother is the female principle of creation and the Lady. She is the goddess of fertility, summer, healing, water, the moon, love, and the seas. The Great Mother held the position of the most magical guide in the Celtic world as she had the "mother finger," which was her index finger. With this finger, the Great Mother could heal, curse, bless you, or guide you down your path.

Herne

Herne is another horned god, also known as Herne the Hunter and the Green Man. He is the god of vine, wild hunt, and vegetation. Once people started to see more deer, they began to celebrate Herne as this was a sign he was coming out of hibernation from the Otherworld. He is associated with the common folk because of his connection with hunting.

Llyr

Llyr is one of the few gods that is believed in by the Irish Celts and Wales. He is the god of the water and the sea. He is the father of Manawyddan, Branwen, and Bran. He was also believed to oversee the Underworld.

Lugh

Lugh is also written as Lugus and is known as the master of skills, such as blacksmithing and working with other crafts. He is associated with the war, reincarnation, journeys, musicians, physicians, healing, initiation, revenge, historians, and prophecy. He is one of the most powerful Celtic gods and is seen as a sun god. The Celts celebrated him for many reasons, such as the light he brought to the world and his connection with crafts and art. His father, Kian (also Cian), was a Tuatha Dé Danann, but Lugh's adoptive father was Manannán mac Lir, who is the god of the sea.

Lugh's most common weapon is the spear of victory, also known as the invincible spear. The spear is extremely hot when it is not in use. It also becomes hotter the longer Lugh uses the spear, allowing it to scorch the earth with its fire.

Macha

Macha is a war goddess. She is known as the Great Queen of the Phantoms and Mother Death. Macha is sometimes called Mana, Minne, Mania, and Mene. Associated with crows, ravens, and other birds, Macha is called upon for magic specific to sexuality, dominance over males, sheer physical force, and fertility.

The Morrighan

The Morrighan is also known as Mórrígan and is the goddess of sovereignty and war. Many Celts referred to her as the "Washer at the Ford" because she could be seen washing a warrior's armor in a stream. Warriors used this as a warning that they would die in battle that day. She is a supreme war goddess and a shape-shifter, meaning she can quickly and easily change her shape. Many referred to her as the Queen of demons and phantoms and the great white goddess. She is associated with witches, night, prophecy, revenge, and night.

She is not always seen as a goddess but as a raven or crow. Celts often saw her in a group of these birds. She is also one of the most complex goddesses in Celtic mythology as some saw her as a triple goddess with her two sisters, Macha and Badb, and other people did not.

Nechtan

Nechtan is the god of the Underworld and associated with Boann. He is the element of earth and is associated with the salmon. The two symbols he is connected to are number nine and wells.

Ogmios

Ogmios is also known as Ogma and compared to Hercules. When written about, he is believed to look like an older version of Hercules that is more tan. However, he is also seen with long chains that run through his mouth. They pierce his tongue, which you often see because of his smile. He is a powerful Celtic god of eloquence who wanted to control as many men as possible and would use his powers of persuasion to do so. Once he had hold of a man, he connected him to his long chain, and it is there the man stayed. If he is not able to persuade someone or he feels attacked in any way, he can use his powers to put a curse on them. Many people believed he would also place a curse on someone who tried to free one of Ogmios's bound men.

Rhiannon

Rhiannon is one of the most well-known Celtic goddesses. She is known as the goddess of the Welsh horse but also plays a vital role in Wales's kingship. She is seen as a great queen and associated with birds as much as horses. She holds power when it comes to the fertility of the Underworld and enchantments. Her husband is the Lord of Dyfed, Pwyll. They married when Rhiannon realized Gwawl tricked her into an engagement. To get out of the engagement, she had to marry the Lord of Dyfed.

Rhiannon and her husband went on to have a baby boy, who was taken one night under the care of his nursemaid. Worried that she would be accused of killing the baby, the nursemaid murdered a puppy and rubbed the blood all over the sleeping face of Rhiannon. Once she woke up, she was accused of killing and eating her child. For forgiveness, she was forced to stand outside the palace walls and tell people who walked by what she did. Pwyll, who never believed his wife killed their son, decided to stand by her the whole time. Fortunately, the couple's baby was returned to them several years later by a lord. He told Rhiannon and Pwyll that he saved their baby from a monster, assumed to be the one who took the baby from his bed. Because the Lord did not know where the baby came from, he decided to raise him himself (Wigington, 2019).

Taliesin

Taliesin is the god of the bards. He is associated with knowledge, wizards, poetry, magic, music, and wisdom. He started his journey as a minor god but worked his way up the ladder to be a more important god because of his knowledge, magic, and wisdom. He is one of the most important gods to the Celtic poets and is believed to give them their gift of writing poetry. To honor him, they wrote about him in their work.

Taranis

Taranis is known as the god of thunder, which is where his name comes from. He is seen as a strong god who holds a lightning bolt and a solar wheel in his hands. Many people in western culture believe that Taranis holds Jupiter in his hands, but the Celts do not agree. Because of his association with lightning, Taranis is connected to fire. He is often praised for the fire in the sky, including the sun. Therefore, he is seen as a Sun God.

Toutatis

Toutatis means the god of the people. He is connected to Esus and Taranis and believed to be a protector of people.

8

THE DRUIDS

The meaning of the Celtic word "Druid" is finding or knowing the oak tree. In the ancient Celtic world, Druids were essential figures in the high-ranking professional class who held occupations as teachers, preachers, and judges. Historically, Druids go back to the 3rd Century BCE. We would not know as much as we do about the Druids if it wasn't for the Roman politician and Dictator Julius Caesar and many mythical tales.

The Druids were known as compelling people who could easily take over tribes that tried to conquer their land. The Druids were considered so powerful that it did not matter what land they wanted to capture because they could have it all, but they were not regarded as greedy. Instead, they wanted to perceive themselves as more peaceful and powerful than anything else.

Part of the reason Druids were considered so powerful is that they continuously trained. It did not matter if they were at the top; they still trained. They prepared for battle and other factors in life so much that they eventually started to train without any weapons at all—and they continued to win one battle after the next. Once the highest Druids realized that battles could be won without weapons, they were not allowed to carry any physical weapons because they believed their words could end hardship and win any battles they had with their enemies.

Another reason the Druids were considered to be extremely powerful is because of their connection to nature. They decided to stop using weapons because of their training, and it gave them a stronger connection to nature, which did not use physical weapons to get what it wanted. Instead of using their strength to work their physical weapons, Druids taught that people needed to use the strength nature gave them.

There was one leader of the Druids, known as the Arch Druid. He had a female that ruled alongside him, and she became known as the High Priestess of the Grove. The Druids wanted to make sure that the Celts received the correct knowledge and education throughout their life, so children were placed in special schools. The schools were separated by gender, and they all studied for several years. Girls and boys were treated equally in these schools, and both genders learned how to fight in battle and run a household. There were very little gender role differences in the Celtic culture, especially when it came to religion.

The Druids were known as an order which had three divisions. The first division was called the Bards. They wore blue robes and were known as poets. The bards were best known as the storytellers of the Druids, and you could compare them to the authors, historians, and scriptwriters of today. In the days of the ancient Celts, they were seen as entertainers, musicians, and lovers of lore who often inspired people to reach into their souls to find their talent.

The Ovates made up the second division and were the philosophers and prophets who wore green robes. You can think of the ovates as the professors of the school, even though all three divisions taught. They were the detective who taught the students to look at the bigger picture of the puzzle and every piece within it. They were the doctor who helped teach them how to heal people, but on a more physical level than the priests. They helped the Celtic children learn how to problem solve, ask questions, and find their direction.

The Druid priests were the third division and wore white robes. While they were considered priests, it is not like how we think of priests in the modern era. Druid priests were more like philosophers, who taught people how to heal themselves and others on a more spiritual level, such as casting and calling forth spirits.

From the three divisions, you can place the bards and ovates into one division and call them the Filid. The priests always stayed in their own division, which makes many people feel they were the most crucial division. All of the Druids in the division were known as teachers, philosophers, and judges. They were seen as advisors to not only children but everyone on their land.

It did not matter if it was a bard who was teaching through music or an ovate who was using different teaching tools, all of them taught the Brehon law, sang Veda hymns, and learned about sacrifice. While there is debate, most of the research reveals that the Celts focused on animals or plant sacrifice instead of humans. This is not to say that human sacrifice did not happen; it is just not as common as many people think.

The Druids also had a social order that they followed to help keep everything organized. This order often followed their occupation but also their religious status. For instance, Druidesses, also known as priestesses, were ranked highly because they held strong magical powers when it comes to herbs, words, crystals, and other stones. They were known to have a sort of compassion for people, especially the sick and dying, that many other gods, goddesses, and even male Druid priests did not have. For example, they would sing the dying to sleep to give them a sense of calmness and let them understand that they are not alone. Some stories state that the priestesses would then help the souls to their location in the Otherworld by calling on certain gods, goddesses, or other entities.

Priestesses were known to show themselves when a mother was about to go into labor. They would remain there for the birth. If the baby did not make it, they would ensure the soul's safe arrival into the next realm and comfort the mother through her next few days. They had the powers to help heal, give prophecies, and were considered sacred.

Another occupation that was high on the social ladder was the blacksmith. One of the biggest reasons for their high order is because they knew how to use all four elements in their work. They made tools by using fire, water, air, and the Earth, which is something that the Celts held in high esteem.

Blacksmiths received training in special magic that other occupations did not. This training took place over a year and one day on a special island. They learned about martial arts and how to heal people with their unique skills. They also learned how to make weapons out of metal, metal magic, and how to fill objects with magic so the weapons would hold special powers when used during battle.

The Celts also learned about and believed in the three concentric circles which represented their existence. The first circle is the Abred, where life comes from. Before the second circle shows, the soul needs to perfect itself for the physical world. The second circle is known as Gwynedd, which is also called purity. In this circle, all good triumphs bad. It is here where reincarnation is prepared. The third circle is known as Ceugant or Infinity. This means that it is the circle where you have the ultimate power.

The soul can only reach the third circle once all lessons have been learned on Earth. Until then, they go from the first to the second circle. When the soul finally reaches their third circle, they do not return to Earth as they have nothing left to learn on the physical world.

As a warning, the Druids wanted everyone to realize that there are ways in which one's soul would never reach the third circle. This happened if you became too arrogant in your life and closed your mind to learning. Another way was by letting your pride take control, telling lies, and reacting in an unnecessarily cruel way to other people.

There were a lot of Celtic festivals, eight to be exact, and these were always celebrated by the highest priests wearing costumes that contained horns. Sometimes they had one horn and other times two. It is necessary to point out that many people, especially in western culture, consider horns to be linked to evil, but this is not the case in the Celtic world. Horns held an extraordinary power and symbolized honoring a certain god or specific skills that gods and goddesses possessed. For example, one horn was used in many fertility celebrations. Horns also symbolized the strength of the male, specifically the god and nature's active side.

One of the most important things to a Druid was that they needed to live in a peaceful world. To people of the modern era, it is not always easy to think of the ancient world as a peaceful place. Because they did not have what we are used to, we imagine them living like cave people, scavenging for food, or freezing in the winter. We believe them dying young from disease or in childbirth. We tend to get the worst images in our heads as we are thankful for the world we live in today. While the images we have are often true for the ancient world, there was more peace than we could ever imagine because this is what the higher-order people and entities wanted for the physical world.

The Celts understood that the higher orders, such as the Druid priests and priestesses, wanted everyone to live in a peaceful world. One way to achieve this was for everyone to follow their direction. The rules, regulations, and laws that the Druids and other higher powers set up for the physical world were there for a reason and most Celts understood this. They went to certain schools that taught them these laws and spiritual beliefs. They learned to live their life in a certain way that taught them to follow the path as this helped keep the peace. This is not to say that the Celts did not have crime or people who broke the law or did not follow the religious beliefs. This happened from time to time, but the Druids took care of the situation when it occurred as they knew the quicker they dealt with the incident, the faster peace would come again.

The Druids spent a lot of time praying and connecting to the Otherworld, which is like their spiritual world. They were highly concerned with how the gods, goddesses, and other spiritual entities felt about their physical world decisions. They understood that their job was to make sure the spiritual entities of the highest realm were pleased with the physical world. They would connect to the entities in many ways, from offering them certain foods to praying. They noted their dreams and often wrote them down to discuss them with other people as they felt that dreams were messages from the spiritual world. Dreams would often bring the answers to their questions.

9

FAIRIES AND FAE FOLK

You have heard of fairies before. You might think of Tinkerbell from Disney's Peter Pan or another beautiful picture of a small woman-type entity with long, flowing hair and broad wings. For generations, fairies have held their place in folklore and are one of the most interesting entities that most people wish were real. However, according to the Celts, they are real. They have a hand in all the magic that happens in the world.

All About Fairies

While most people see fairies as friendly, helpful, and magical, they can also come off as cruel and hateful. At least, this is the way the Celts saw them. Another big difference between the modern-day version of fairies and what the Celts thought is their size. In the ancient world, they were seen more like angels. They were anywhere from tall and beautiful human-like creatures to small, monster-like entities. A fairy could measure anywhere from 18 inches to over four feet tall. Some were even considered to grow taller than four feet and stand above any human.

Fairies had their favorite colors, which were green and red, and were usually shown in their clothing. For instance, the female fairies wore red shoes with a green dress. They would also dress themselves up with jewelry, such as pearls or a type of crystal. Male fairies wore yellow pants with green or red shirts. Some male fairies wore other colors, such as white or blue, and happened to dress similar to the country they came from.

If a fairy wanted to live a happy and disease-free life, they needed sleep and food. They often received food from the offerings laid out during the night from the Celts or the feasts. If they did not take care of themselves, they would become sick and die. They could also become weak, and they were a target for a beast or monster to kill.

Fairies often had a good time within their communities through dances and music. Many were musically talented and often seen with an instrument, such as a harp. They also played the bagpipes, whistles, cymbals, drums, and tambourines. There is a chance that we do not know any fairy's real name because the legend states they hid this from humans by giving a fake name. They were also known as incredibly generous, compassionate, neat, good at keeping a secret and loving to care for babies. Many fairies would bring in freshwater during the night, so the baby would have that when they woke up.

Celtic mythology described the fairies as a race who went into hiding because they were frightened by some sort of unknown force. One story said that the Tuatha Dé Danann forced them into the underworld after they won the first war and officially became the rulers of Ireland. But there were other worlds that the fairies could have run to, such as the Land of the Youth, Pleasant Plain, or the Isle of Women. Some people felt that they often hide in trees, and some thought that they were the reason for the wind. They would come out at night or when called upon to help but remained quiet so they would not awake the beasts that once sent them into hiding.

Some fairies prefer to live alone, but many will live in little villages or a group. Celts could tell who was a lone fairy vs. a community fairy by their clothing. Fairies who live with others dress in a grand way while lone fairies will wear leaves, cobwebs, flowers, or green moss.

Fairies have several characteristics that they are known for, such as troublemaking and protecting people. How they act will depend on what type of fairy they are. For example, the Banshee is considered the fairy of death, and the Pooka is a shape-shifter that people are known to fear because of the horrid forms it takes at night. Other characteristics that are attributed to fairies throughout folklore are kidnapping babies and leaving changelings instead, healing powers, and playing harmless pranks that were meant to be more fun than anything else.

Fairies are also known to curse people who hurt their land. Even the sweet and caring ones will seek revenge on someone that hurts their tree, meadows, bodies of water, or wherever else they decide to live. The revenge they sought was usually cursing the person and their descendants who caused the harm. People became so afraid of these curses and the bad luck that would come to their family that they refused to touch parts of the land where the fairies lived. For example, they would not tear down some trees to build homes or businesses.

People took time to offer the fairies foods, flowers, and other objects they liked as this would bring and leave them in good spirits. This way, they were less likely to cause too much mischief or harm when they came to the physical world. Some of the offerings included milk, chocolate, cake, and other sweets. Sometimes items that were shiny, like metals and crystals, were left. Because fairies were seen as colorful beings, the Celts believed they enjoyed objects of color.

The Banshee

The Banshee is one type of fairy that was feared, but not because she would harm people. She warned people that harm was coming their way, one way or another. She was known as an omen of death. The legend states that she would appear to people and often start screaming, to the point of screeching, in their face. She gave a high-pitched scream to ensure that you heard her. While people knew she meant death was coming to their family, they were never sure who the person was. Sometimes she showed up to the person who died, and other times she showed to a different family member.

While there are a few depictions of the Banshee, she is usually drawn with long white hair and a ghostly pale expression. There are times where she is seen with bloodstained clothes. Some Celts believed if they saw blood on her dress, it meant that someone would die in an accident or be murdered. If her dress did not have blood, they were to die of illness or natural causes.

Even though the Banshee is one of the most well-known fae folk, she is hardly written about in texts. One example comes from King James I of Scotland, who stated he saw a pale woman with long white hair wailing at him. He did not explain the wailing as a scream, but more like a painful cry, like a mother who just found out her child had died. Not too long after James saw the wailing woman, the Earl of Atholl passed away. Most people believe the death happens within 24 hours, but no one can be sure if this timeline is correct or not.

The Pooka

The Pooka, also known as Puka, is another fairy that did not have the best reputation in the Celtic world. While some believe the Pooka is female, most stories place him as a male. He is feared because he can turn into hideous monsters during the night. Not only can he change into a bat, but also dogs, black horses, or goats. Sometimes he takes the form of such horrible beasts that people fear they saw a demon. Most stories focus on the negativity surrounding Pooka, stating that he goes around destroying people's crops and homes, and killing livestock while they sleep. Fortunately, not all stories are bad.

The Pooka might show up as a frightening animal, but he is more likely he will help you than hurt you. For example, the fairy was known to help one Celt by giving them a life of luck with wealth and happiness. To thank Pooka, they designed clothing and left them for the fairy to take back with him.

The Merrow

The merrow is similar to mermaids, which is precisely where they get their name from. While they were rarely seen or written about, people do know that they are a bit frightening to look at. In other words, they do not look like Ariel from Disney's The Little Mermaid. Instead, they are portrayed with long pointy ears with very pointy teeth. Some people state they saw them with a fishtail while other people say they have legs and can walk on land. The way to explain the swimming with legs is that they have unique clothes that takes them through the water's currents.

Some myths state that the merrow can turn herself into a beautiful human when she wants to walk on land. They have to hide pieces of the sea form, which was often taken by fishermen. Once a fisherman saw the merrow looking for her swimming gear, they would lure her into their home and try to capture her. Of course, she was usually able to escape, and this meant that the fisherman needed to watch his back because the marrow would seek revenge.

Changelings

Changelings are a famous fairy tale that is mainly attributed to Europe. A changeling is a sickly or deformed child who was abandoned by their parents. The legend goes that the changeling replaced a baby. The fairies who made the swap kidnapped the child and brought them back to their land. Some changelings were always crying while others could barely hear or make a sound.

It is hard to understand the legend of a changeling, but many people feel that it became a way to explain why babies suddenly fell ill overnight. It often happened that parents would lay their baby down for the night, and when they went to wake them up in the morning, their baby was unwell. The changeling was also used to explain why children acted strangely or turned rebellious. If the Celts felt that their child was taken by a fairy and replaced with a changeling, they would place the baby above the fire and say a chant. If the baby ran off, then it was a changeling, and the real baby would return to their home.

Leprechauns

Leprechauns are a mythical figure that most people have heard of. You think of them as looking for their pot of gold or being associated with wealth in some way. However, what they do not always realize is that leprechauns are known as a fairy. They are usually seen as mischievous and even a little bad or evil. They are also known to creep into homes and businesses during the night and make shoes. Described as wearing green suits and being incredibly tiny, it is easy for them to sneak in and out without being noticed. Some stories paint their skin as green while others give them a more tan or pale color. Some stories have leprechauns hiding treasure to help people in need of a financial boost or other means.

One little unknown belief about leprechauns is that if you were able to capture them, they would have to grant you three wishes as long as you set him free. Some people state that this was a trick, and they never granted three wishes while others say that they kept their word.

The Dullahan

The Dullahan was another type of fairy that was well-known in ancient Celtic culture but often stayed in the rural parts of Ireland. He was most likely to come out during festivals around midnight. He is seen as a ghost-like horseman with a black cloak. People often heard him galloping and snorting. One of the most terrifying thing about the Dullahan is he carries his head with him. Because the head looks like it is made from stale bread or old cheese, he carries a smell with him that is seen as a warning sign that he is on his way. He carries a whip with him that is made out of a human spine, and when the horse charges, you can see fire or sparks coming from his nose.

Like the Banshee, the Dallahan is known as a warning sign that death will come to your home. However, he just stares at the house where someone is about to die, so it is not always known who will be death's next victim.

The Grogoch

The grogoch is a half-human and a half fairy-like creature who came to Ireland from Scotland. They are described as elderly with a coat and red hair, and small in stature. They are known to be extremely dirty as they wear twigs and dirt instead of clothing. They are both male and female, but most people reported seeing female grogoches.

No matter what their appearance is, grogoches have a lot of power and can quickly make themselves invisible to the world. They will not show themselves to anyone unless they feel they can trust you. They live in caves and have a very little problem with the changing seasons of Ireland.

Grogoches are known as shy fairies, but they like helping people in certain areas. They love the outdoors and enjoy gardening. Trustworthy people usually see them while they are gardening and become frightened because of their appearance. However, the legend states that they are nothing to be afraid of because they simply want to help you with your gardening so that you can grow the best flowers, plants, and vegetables. Once they become comfortable around humans, they are anything but shy. They will spend their day helping and talking to people that they trust. It is stated that some Celts used to become a little annoyed with these little fairies and ask them to leave. While they would leave, they would feel and look hurt. Typically, they would not show themselves to you again because they did not trust you anymore and did not want to become a bother.

Other Fairies

Other fairies and fae folk that are often not discussed in Celtic mythology include the Brownie, who also goes by Bwbadchod or Bwca. They are known to dress in brown clothes, have shaggy hair, brown faces, and be only about three feet high. They are known to sneak into homes during the night and help people by finishing their work. However, brownies will not just go to any house. They divide themselves to choose houses that become their responsibility. This means that one brownie cannot go into the home of another brownie.

Brownies will not complete their work for free. They request to have cake, and a bowl of cream or milk left out every night for their energy and as thanks. If they do not receive this, they will not finish the work and might leave the home altogether. They might also seek revenge by becoming mischievous, which also happens when they feel left out or offended.

10

THE OTHERWORLD

The Otherworld has several names attached to it, and what name a Celt used would depend on where they lived and the group they associated with. Some of the names include Annwn, Tech Duinn, Emain, Mag Mell, and Avalon. Some Celts believed that more than one Otherworld existed, and each had its own name. For instance, the spirits of the dead lived in one world, while the fairies lived in another.

The Otherworld was the Celtic way of saying that there was an afterlife. Their souls would continue into the next realm where they would wait until their future life. Of course, if the soul learned everything it needed to in the physical world, then it no longer needed to come back to the physical world as a human. Instead, it could remain a spirit forever, watching over their next of kin or continuing to grow on its spiritual path. For most souls, they returned to Earth in a new body, with a new family, and a new mission that would continue to lead them down their path and help them learn lessons. But there was also a possibility that the soul would not reincarnate into a new body.

They might become an animal or even a plant. The Celts believed that every living entity from flowers to humans had a soul. This soul could take any living form as it had many lessons to learn.

The Otherworld had to exist for the Celts because they believed the soul was immortal. Even though there are mythical legends of gods and goddesses dying, the soul itself could not die. But, the soul could take the wrong path in its life and never learn the lessons it should. When this happens, the queen of the Otherworld will not allow the soul entry into the realm. Instead, they will continue to walk in the physical world or go into a different realm, one that was meant for the negative entities, demons, and other evil souls.

There are also stories where the Celts believed that the soul could reach a higher realm. This is thought to if they believed in more than one Otherworld, which most groups and villages did. This happens when your soul continues to walk its rightful path and proves to the gods and goddesses that it is worthy of praise. The ultimate destination for a soul is to reach the highest realm, which is the location souls go when they have learned everything they needed to and no longer need to live in the physical world. Many people would see this as a heaven-like realm where you can leave if someone gives you offerings in the physical world, but otherwise, you remain in your realm for eternity.

The Celts believed there was an Otherworld where human spirits went once they left a body and where the gods and goddesses lived when they were not on Earth. In mythology, it is described as a realm where spirits will obtain beauty and forever look young. They will have plenty of joy in the Otherworld and always feel like everything is abundant. There is nothing any spirit or deity needs to ask for in this realm because everything is automatically provided simply with a thought.

One of the most significant factors is that a spirit needed permission to enter the Otherworld. They could not merely walk in just because they passed on. The same went for any gods, goddesses, and other mythical creatures of the Celtic culture. While the Otherworld was welcoming, it was possible to be turned away if you committed a crime as a human, or your spirit did something wrong.

A mythical hero, fairy, or other spiritual entity can visit the Otherworld without having to stay there. This happens when a spirit who remains in the Otherworld invites them in. For instance, if a person dies and their soul moves into the realm, they can invite any god, goddess, or fairy they want to visit them. However, once the visit is over and the spirit has their answer or what they need, the mythical figure needs to leave the world and go back into the physical world or their realm.

Just as mythical entities need to be invited into the Otherworld, spirits from this world need to be invited into the physical world. For example, if the Celts had one of their festivals coming up and they wanted to invite relatives who have passed on, fairies, or any other entity, they would place an offering in their home or the community. This offering was considered an invitation to the spiritual entity that they could use to enter the physical world for the festivities or another reason. Some of the offerings included fresh fruit, flowers, crafts, and other food.

They felt that for a soul to gain entry into the Otherworld, they would receive a silver branch from the sacred apple tree. Sometimes there was an apple on the branch, and other stories state that all the soul needed to be was to carry an apple into the other realm. This silver branch or apple was considered to be the ticket or passport for entry. Once the soul came to the entry of the other realm, they needed to show the queen the gift they had. According to the legend, this usually happened within the first hour or two after death. Once the branch or apple was given to the queen, she would let the soul into the Otherworld.

No one truly knows the location of the Otherworld. The ancient Celts had an idea, but they could never be sure. All they knew was that for a spirit to go or visit this world, they had to go through a cave or underwater. There were many points of entry, and each mythical hero had their own entry location. For instance, a goddess connected to water might go underwater or through a particular stream to get to the other realm where fairies who are said to live in caves would find their entry point in the caves or mountains.

There are also Celtic beliefs that stated the world of spirits exists among the physical world. They claimed it was not always easy to notice that the two worlds remained side by side. Still, people living in the physical world could tell by paying attention to the pressure in the air, the temperature, and magical mist, or seeing a spiritual animal.

One of the most common beliefs, according to most Celts, when it came to the location of the Otherworld, is that it was found amid the Western Ocean. Similar to the physical world, it had rulers and a social order. For instance, gods and goddesses were at the top of the order, and then there were fairies. Human souls would be slated for near the bottom of the ladder.

When it comes to what the other realm looked like, it was up to the Celt's imagination. Some stated that it was the most beautiful place and full of peaceful scenes of nature, such as mountains and rivers. Other people believed that it was full of light as the sun never disappeared. Some even imagined that you would walk through the realm and see all the fairies, gods, goddesses, and other spirits that were in the world. No one was invisible in this world. The spirits could even see the human world and everything that was going on.

11

THE TREE OF LIFE

You have probably seen the symbol for the tree of life several times, as it is often found on jewelry and decorations. For the ancient Celts, the tree gave them a sense of harmony and peace. Part of this is because their sacred gods and goddesses lived among the trees. Another reason was they needed trees to live, as trees kept them warm, could be used to cook their food, and so much more. Celts spend their days thanking the spirits for the goodness they received in their lives as they focused on the positive over the negative. Therefore, many praised the gods and goddesses for their homes daily.

Another reason they celebrated trees is that they would not have homes without trees. Think of the forests. How many trees give homes to life, from the ancient Celts to the animals and the spirits. As the symbol of the tree of life is a circle, so is the life it gives other people. It creates a part of the cycle of life that is necessary for survival.

Celts believed the tree of life not only gave people life, but it also had magical powers. Whenever they cleared land for a field, home, or a farm, they would make sure to plant a big tree in the center. This tree became a meeting place as they gathered together to celebrate festivals, play games, and talk. Everything of importance that happened in their lives occurred around the main tree. Without caring for this tree and giving it life by spending time near the tree, it would not grow. Therefore, they would not receive the food or housing they needed to live.

The tree was so sacred to the Celts that anyone caught chopping down a tree faced grave punishment. If the person survived the punishment for the crime, they would remain an enemy of their area.

Sacred Animals

Every animal had a special meaning in the Celtic world. Some of the animals were seen as warning signs, while others were held in high esteem and regarded as sacred. They also believed that spirits could take the form of animals for various reasons. For example, the goddess of Sovereignty was seen as a bear, cow, and horse.

The horse is seen all over history and myths. To the Celts, the horse had a unique magical power that linked them to many gods and goddesses, such as Epona and Macha. During times of war, horses gave them the strength to fight. They were also seen as a form of transportation, especially if someone needed to get somewhere quickly.

Bears were found in many totem Celtic designs and were often referred to as "arth." They found the bears to be sacred because they showed strength and focus. They could handle a lot of pressure and sustain themselves under tough circumstances. Bears had a place in the Celtic world because they needed the power to create peace in their lives.

Dogs are recognized as one of the most sacred animals. Sometimes called hounds, they are devoted friends but could also bring punishments to those who deserve it. The Underworld Hounds were known as the punishers and perceived as white with red ears. However, they never prayed on the innocent, only the guilty. Many people believed that if someone guilty of a crime received a verdict of innocent, the Underworld Hounds would come to ensure they received their punishment. While some people see the Underworld Hounds as vicious, most Celts believed that they took care of the earthly people and saw them as devoted dogs. Another reason dogs were sacred to the Celts is because of their instinct and ability to scent a trail.

Cows and bulls were viewed as a symbol of land and considered to hold wealth. Celts often praised the cows and asked for their help and guidance when it came to farming their land and receiving goods for their services. One reason they saw cows as so sacred is because of all the supplies they could get from the animal, such as food, milk, and hides to keep them warm. Many gods and goddesses turned into a cow or bull or kept one with them. For example, the river goddess, Boand, was seen as a cow. She was seen as a goddess that provided milk to the Celts.

Crows and other birds were other sacred animals. While there were a lot of birds, and each had their distinguishing features, the Celts did not distinguish between them. They believed that they all held the same powers and goodness. Birds were seen in two different ways. First, they were seen as hunters who held magical powers in times of war. When the Celts needed to fight in battle, they would call on the birds, specifically the crow and raven. They started associating birds with the battlefield because they would be seen eating the flesh off the enemy's corpse. Another way birds were used included telling the future.

Celts believed that most birds could say to the future and would alert them of any bad news through warnings. Birds would come to a person in their dreams to help them make the right choices for their future. It was also believed that birds would predict the end of the world, allowing the Celts to prepare.

The goddess Brigid owned a **Boar**, who was considered a sacred animal. The boar shows up in a lot of ancient texts, tales, and myths. It shows bravery and royalty. When they were in battle, the Celts turned to the boar to help them in their fight. Many soldiers drew pictures of a boar onto their supplies. They believed that it kept the spirit of the animal near them at all times. They were also placed on some of the most valuable pieces of the Celtic world, such as bronze coins and gold.

Salmon are another sacred animal that is associated with Celtic magic. The salmon held a lot of knowledge when it came to spells and other forms of magic. Celts often called on this animal to help them with their magic. It is also connected to the spiritual world as it was considered a doorway to the Otherworld. The salmon is also unique because it is seen as the wisest and oldest of all the animals.

Sacred Places

One of the most sacred places relating to the ancient Celts is the **Hill of Tara**. It is located between Dunshaughlin and Navan in County Meath, Leinster, Ireland. According to legend, it is where the king of Ireland would go when it came time to take his throne. Most of the rituals which included the king took place on this hill.

The Holy Island, or the Inis Cealtra, is another sacred place that people continue to visit today. It holds a round tower along with what is left of six sacred churches that once stood on the island.

The Ridgeway and Avebury are other sacred places of the ancient Celts. The Ridgeway is known as one of the oldest roads in Europe. It holds the sacred image of the goddess of the land. Avebury has double rows of grey stones that people used as a way for direction.

Stonehenge is another sacred place and one that most people know about. It is one of the most popular tourist destinations because it is from ancient times, and while many people have an opinion of what it once was used for, no one is 100% sure.

12

CELTIC FESTIVALS

For the ancient Celts, the Wheel of the Year represented the cyclical changes of the seasonal festivals. These festivals are known as religious celebrations and correspond with the seasonal changes, such as the Winter Solstice and the Spring Equinox. They signal a significant change in the weather, including the length of daylight and nighttime. For example, the Celts celebrated the Summer Solstice because it is the longest day of the year.

One of the more magical beliefs the Celts held with the Wheel of the Year is that everything continued. Of course, the years changed in number, and people died, but this did not mean that everyone or anything remained lost in time. The natural cycle of the physical and spiritual world would repeat, meaning that through one way or another, everything would come back. This is one of the biggest reasons the Celts celebrated the changing of the seasons. It was a time where one season made its complete cycle and came back into their lives.

The Celts celebrated a total of eight festivals throughout the year. With each celebration was a day full of events with at least one main event. These moments were a time of prayer, giving thanks, and excitement for the future. Each holiday allowed the Celts to let go of their past and focus on a new beginning. This is what nature intended for them to do. They celebrated by coming out of whatever darkness they felt tied to and walking toward the light. If they remained in the night, they committed one of the worst sins possible—the gateway sin. Holding on to this sin made people feel resentment and bitterness. They felt a great sense of self-pity that did not allow them to walk toward the path of light.

Winter Solstice

The Winter Solstice or Yule festival took place from December 20th through 23rd. Another name for it is Alban Arthan. While the Yule is not the most important festival in the ancient Celtic world, it is considered one of the turning points of the year as it is the shortest day. It marks the day where there is more darkness than light, but the sun's light will continue to increase every day until the Summer Solstice. Many activities were celebrated during the Winter Solstice, but the everyday activities included sacrifices, gift exchanges, and feasting. Today, many historians compare the Yule to Christmas, which is often celebrated by Christians.

During the Yule, Celts decorated an evergreen tree outside to honor the spirits and deities, who lived in the trees. The decorated tree was the Celt's way to say "thank you" to the spirits, gods, and goddesses for all the luck and gifts they sent to the physical world throughout the year. A special thanks were sent to the Oak King. The Oak King ruled during the earth as the days started to become longer.

Another part of the Yule celebration included a bonfire with a Yule log. The fire was important because it was the symbol of new beginnings and light. They threw items, such as holly, into the fire as a way to welcome the new beginnings and let go of the past. They would hold hands and sing songs about the fire. At the end of the festival, they would save a piece of the Yule log, which helped start the fire for the following year.

Imbolc

Imbolc is also known as Candlemas and falls on February 1st. This festival celebrates the midpoint between winter and spring and the rebirth of purification. It is connected to fertility and pregnancy, giving the Celts hope for growing their family in the coming year. The Celts believe this festival honors new beginnings and will often release any negativity from the past and rededicate themselves for the new year.

Imbolc is observed at the same time as Groundhog Day and is known as a fire and light festival with a special celebration to Brigid, the hearth goddess. As a goddess, Brigid focused on fertility, medicine, and poetry. People would weave dolls into Brigid out of corn stalks to honor her. In return, Brigid would ensure that the Celts received good luck throughout the year.

Ostara

Ostara is also known as Alban Eilir, which means the Light of the Earth. This celebration runs from March 20th to 23rd. The Celts used it to celebrate new beginnings with the Spring Equinox. When they first started celebrating Ostara, they considered it a holy day and did very little festivities. However, this slowly changed over time, eventually becoming linked to the egg and rabbit. The Celts saw it is a special time because the day and night are now equal, and light is about to take over darkness.

Eostre is the goddess associated with Ostara. She is known as the mother of the dawn and also linked to fertility. The legend goes that Eostre has been hibernating during the winter and is now up and ready to bring the next Yule into the world. Like other celebrations, festivities filled the streets for the Celts as they ate foods that include rabbits and eggs. They also decorated their homes with colorful flowers to give a little light to the new beginnings.

Beltane

Beltane is a festival that occurs on May 1st. You might know this festival as May Day, which is another name for this celebration. Beltane comes from the sun god, Bel, which means "a bright fire." Because this is known as a fire festival, the Celts celebrated with a big bonfire and dancing around a tree. While dancing, they decorated the tree, sometimes called a maypole, with long ribbons and flowers. This symbolized the awakening of nature for a new year as the days started to become lighter. It was important for the head of the household to attach a branch to the ceiling above the table, so fairies protected the family. The Celts did not view the fairies as evil but as jokesters who would play tricks on the family members if they did not defend themselves. Another part of the ritual to protect themselves included lighting a candle and cleansing their home. They started on the floor by the front door moving the candles around the door, each window, and all corners of their home.

The Celts celebrated fertility, the coming of summer, light, passion, and desires. People talked about what they wanted to do and believed they could achieve it, as long as they stayed close to the spirits because they held the magical powers.

Litha

Litha is one of the Celts favorite celebrations that falls on the Summer Solstice. This is around the longest day of the year, and they celebrate it from June 20th to 23rd. It is when the Oak King surrenders his title to his brother, the Holly King. The

Celts believe this festival is special because it is the day of the year where light triumphs darkness. Litha is sometimes referred to as Alban Hefin, which means the Light of the Shore.

Like other festivals, Litha is celebrated with a feast, bonfire, and dancing. The Celts focused on eating fresh fruits and honey cakes. They performed rituals to protect themselves from negative entities that came with the Beltane celebration. Many Celts also created sun wheels and hung them around their home for added protection. Another part of the festival included marriages. June is known as the best month to marry, at least for ancient Celts, and many decided to marry during Litha. If this happened, they needed extra protection to make sure that their marriage remained safe and happy.

Lughnasadh

Lughnasadh occurs on August 1st and was a fire festival that celebrated the first harvest of the season. It marked the seasons turning from summer to fall and called for truth from the god Lugh. Celts viewed Lugh as one of the most important spirits and felt he was more like a hero because you need a harvest to put food on your table. Celts offered their gods and goddesses fresh fruit during this celebration but paid particular attention to Lugh.

According to ancient legend, Lugh had a mother named Tailtiu, who was one of the earliest goddesses. Needing to provide for her son and community, she worked endlessly in her field to plow the harvest. As a result, she died from exhaustion. During her funeral, Lugh celebrated her life through sacrifice and a feast. The following year, Lugh decided to continue honoring his mother through celebrating the harvest with a feast and several other activities, such as archery competitions, races, fencing matches, and wrestling matches. Celts continued to celebrate Lughnasadh because they felt it ensured the harvest continued in the next year.

Mabon

Mabon celebrates the second harvest and is a time to give thanks. It did not matter what the Celts lost or gained during that year. They gave thanks for their blessings and their mistakes. It was often called Alban Elfed, which means Light of the Water. It was celebrated from September 21st through 24th when the days and nights are equal, and night will grow a bit longer every day.

While all gods and goddesses are celebrated during the festival, they mainly focused on Cernnunos, the fertility god. The Celts believed that Cernnunos went into the underworld at this time and returned in the spring. He was celebrated through a feast and other activities.

Samhain

Samhain was celebrated on November 1st and was the most important festival of the year. To the Celts, it was identified as the beginning of a new year. This celebration said goodbye to summer and the long days of light. It welcomed the darker seasons, but this is not to be taken negatively. When people think of darkness, they think of evil and coldness, but this is not what the Celts felt. They believed that darkness is part of the physical world, and they had to go through darkness to get to the light. Therefore, welcoming darkness back into their lives meant that light would soon show itself.

Another essential factor of Samhain was that it connected the living with the dead. While many cultures did not talk freely about this concept in ancient times, the Celts believed that after someone died, they went to the part of the world called the "in-between." This is a world, similar to purgatory, where souls stay until they can fully transition. The Celts also believed that once a spirit passed on, they could come back into the physical world and visit during this festival. Therefore, they prepared the favorite meal of their ancestors and also left treats for other spirits. Unfortunately, this was not always a pleasant experience. If someone wronged a family member of the departed, the spirit would come and seek revenge on the person.

13

CORRESPONDENCES

The following sections will give you a list of colors, elements, candles, and other items used in spells. All of the lists will reveal what certain types or colors mean, so you know which one to use when you start working your magic. You must ensure you follow your spell and apply the corresponding color candle, element, or incense as your spell can turn sour if you use something that you were not supposed to. Luckily, there is nothing to worry about as long as you follow the lists and spell. You also want to make sure that you cast your circle and close it out at the end correctly. Another tip is never to forget to thank your higher powers that helped you as they will remember who thanks them and who does not.

Elements

Each element has its own characteristics, rulers, colors, and magical tools. This is a guide to help you as you continue your path of magic.

The Element of Fire is ruled by firedrakes, salamanders, and the flame. Its king is Djin, and its colors are red and white. The symbols of fire include rainbows, volcanoes, stars, and the sun. The magical tools to use when you are casting are a lamp, candles, writing down requests on paper, burning of herbs, and a dagger. It is attracted by incense, candles, lamps, and fire. The best times to perform a ritual is during the summer and at noon. You will ask for change, perceptions, learning, passion, authority, energy, purification, freedom, sight, illumination, love, sexuality, and healing.

The Element of Earth is ruled by trolls, gnomes, and dwarfs who are an inner part of the earth. They are intensely attuned to the minerals, gems, and other items of the earth. The king of the earth is Ghom, also written as Gob or Ghob, and powders and salts attract this element. The magical tools associated are salt, stones, trees, cord magic, the pentagram, images, and gems. Green or black are the colors, and the symbols are mountains, fields, mines, soil, plains, rocks, caves, and gemstones. The best time to perform a ritual focusing on the earth element is at midnight or anytime during the night. The type of rituals you will cast include surrendering your self-will and requesting an increase in riches, money, success, fertility, treasures, business, stability, and prosperity. You can also use the earth to help you find a job, start a business, and get in touch with your empathic abilities.

The Element of Water is ruled by mermaids, mermen, streams, seas, lakes, springs, ponds, fairies that live in the water, undines, and nymphs. Its king is Necksa, and it is attracted to solutions and water. The magical tools used are a goblet, the sea, a cauldron, and mirrors. The two primary colors to use are blue or gray. Its symbols are rivers, pools, fog, rain, springs, lakes, wells, and mist. The best time to cast magic is during the fall and sunset. You will ask for emotions, purification, love, pleasure, marriage, happiness, dreams, sleep, psychic abilities, focus on your sense of smell and states, plants, healing, improving your subconscious mind, and friendships.

The Element of Air is ruled by fairies who live in the trees, mountains, or flowers. Zephyrs and Sylphs also govern it. Its king is Paralda and incenses, and oils attract it. The best type of ritual to cast with air is for knowledge, hearing, inspiration, happiness, peace, ideas, freedom, finding out the truth, finding items that are lost, and psychic abilities. You want to use the element of air if you are about to travel as it can help keep you safe. The best time to perform your magic is during the sunrise and spring. Its symbols are the clouds, breath, plants, trees, sky, wind, vibration, herbs, and flowers. The magical tools to use are incense, your creative imagination, and a wand. The two colors air associates with are yellow and red.

Colors of Candles

It is always necessary to recognize that each color of a candle corresponds to a certain feeling or something you want to work on. For example, if you're going to focus on your health, you will want to light a red candle. However, red candles also bring out sexual sensations, so you always want to ensure that you are clear in what you are asking your higher powers to help you with when lighting the candle and casting a spell.

Green candles are best if you want to focus on good luck, generosity, money, success, balance, marriage, abundance, wealth, and fertility.

White candles are known to symbolize spirituality, purity, truth, power of a higher nature, sincerity, and wholeness.

Purple candles are best if you want to strengthen your psychic abilities, increase spiritual contact, or work on your success. Other reasons to light a purple candle include idealism, wisdom, protection, and progress.

Indigo candles symbolize neutralizing another person's magic, stopping gossip, stopping lies, meditation, and balancing out karma.

Red candles are known to help increase your courage, willpower, health, energy, or strength. You can also overcome your laziness and any fear you feel by lighting a red candle.

Yellow candles are best known for the power of the mind, confidence, action, concentration, sudden changes, intellect, creativity, gentle persuasion, imagination, attraction, and inspiration.

Brown candles are known to attract money and give you financial success. They also help with balance, influence the earth elemental, help you study, and increase concentration and intuition.

Silver or Very Light Gray candles symbolize victory, meditation, stability, psychic abilities, removal of negative energy, and female deity powers.

Blue candles are known for inspiration, patience, bringing harmony into your environment, protection, peace, happiness, good health, truth, fidelity, and occult power.

Very Light Yellow or Gold candles will strengthen your intuition, divination, financial benefits, male deity powers, great fortune, and understanding.

Lighting a **Pink** candle focuses on affection, love, romance, healing of the spirit, spiritual awakening, togetherness, and love.

When you light a **Black** candle, you are reversing negative energies, binding negative entities, protecting, and releasing negative thoughts and dark magic.

An **Orange** candle helps when it comes to stimulation, encouragement, sudden changes, power, control, change luck, and adaptability.

Magenta candles symbolize quick changes and increase the speed that other candles work. Therefore, magenta is often burned with another color candle.

Incense

While incense is easier to find than it used to be, many people still want to find the best place to get their incense for their magic. If you live in a rural area, do not trust online shopping, or if you want to make your incense, here is a great list to help you.

Are you trying to meditate more in your life, but you find yourself a bit stuck? Do you find your mind getting lost in thoughts, or you simply feel too busy to take 10 to 15 minutes out of your day, especially in the morning, to meditate? If you want to meditate, the best incense to look for includes bay, wisteria myrrh, nutmeg, frankincense, acacia, cinnamon, and angelica.

To create balance in your life, your spells, or help someone find balance in their life, you want to use orange, jasmine, or rose.

To boost your creativity, you want to use wild cherry, lotus, honeysuckle, rose, savory, or vervain.

Several types of incense are great when it comes to anointing. Most people will use oils to anoint, which is fine, but you can also use incense. All you need to do is rub one of these types on a candle, crystal, or any object that you are using in your spellwork. Some people will anoint with an incense stick by lighting it and then circling the object with the smoke. You can use angelica, frankincense, lavender, jasmine, lily of the valley, acacia, carnation, lotus, rose, vervain, or rosemary.

To give a blessing or call for a blessing, you can use frankincense, elder, carnation, lotus, rue, cypress, or rosemary.

Do you have a problem when it comes to swearing, and you want to stop? You might know of someone who has a problem cursing, especially when it is not appropriate. In this case, you want to find the following incense: elder, blackthorn, or pepper.

Banishing is popular in spellwork and is something that many people do. In fact, for people who use magic regularly, they will usually banish any negative energy quarterly or twice a year. Sometimes people will notice a change in their home before they think of banishing. To banish, some of the best types include clove, rose, violet, elder, mugwort, vervain, cedar, patchouli, betony, and yarrow.

Exorcism is a word we all know, and it is something that scares many people when they get into magic and the spiritual world. While many images you have in your mind come from Hollywood movies, it is possible to have a negative entity attach itself to you. If they become too attached, they will take over your body, and you will then need some type of exorcism. When this happens, priests or other people who perform exorcisms will use frankincense, myrrh, rosemary, basil, fern, pepper, wormwood, bay, lavender, pine, or mullein during the exorcism. Sometimes a combination of some of these incense types will be used for better protection and strength.

It is always a great idea to cleanse and purify your items or yourself. This is something you should always do before you cast any magic. To do this with incense, you want to look for laurel, lavender, rosemary, basil, cedar, elder, dragon's blood, valerian, thyme, woodruff, burdock, rue, peppermint, salt, betony, and hyssop.

The best types of incense to improve your visions are frankincense, acacia, marigold, wormwood, mugwort, dittany of Crete, and bay.

Courage and determination are something that we all need a little increase in now and then. You might need the courage to start a new job or commitment to see a project through. No matter what you need in this area, some of the best incense to choose are allspice, rosemary, mullein, musk, and dragon's blood.

Changes are not easy for anyone, and people sometimes need help when it comes to significant life changes. If this seems like you or someone you know, dragon's blood, peppermint, or woodruff are some of your best choices.

To work on binding, you want to use apple, dragon's blood, cypress, pepper, wormwood, rowan, or cayenne.

It seems we live in a world where we always lack some type of energy, strength, or power. Whatever you feel needs a boost in your life, the best incense to look for are frankincense, musk, allspice, carnation, lotus, bay, cinnamon, dragon's blood, oak, verbena, thyme, and holly.

To build your clairvoyance, you want to use lilac, eyebright, marigold, cinnamon, laurel, honeysuckle, acacia, rose, wormwood, thyme, mugwort, hazel, rowan, or dittany of Crete.

People are always looking for more good luck and fortune. Sometimes something happens in your life, and you are seeking justice. In any of these cases, some of the best incense to light is mint, violet, nutmeg, cinnamon, bayberry, cedar, or lotus.

The two types of incense to increase your willpower are St. John's-wort and rosemary.

Inspiration and wisdom are something that can help out everyone. To build this area in your life, you want to choose rue, reed, lily of the valley, oakmoss, rosemary, clove, rowan, fir, laurel, cinquefoil, or cypress.

New beginnings are something that people are always looking forward to. Whether it is a new job, a new chapter in your life, or trying to start anew by working harder toward your goals, several types of incense can help you. One of the most useful and most reliable types is birch oil.

Love always seems to be in the air for someone. Whether it is soon Valentine's day, spring, and you notice everyone is getting engaged, or you see a couple planning their wedding, everyone wants to find that special person and feel loved. However, there are many different versions of love, so it is important not to get too caught up in one type. If you are looking for more love in your life, you want to choose apple blossom, gardenia, musk, catnip, heather, lavender, marigold, mistletoe, savory, valerian, vanilla, jasmine, or rose.

To open your psychic centers a little more, you want to make sure you have lotus, mimosa, nutmeg, mugwort, or wisteria on hand.

If you are looking into reincarnation, you want to have either sandalwood or lilac.

In this world, it seems that we can never have enough defense or protection. If you need this, or you want to focus on protecting someone else, there are several types of incense you can try. For example, you can choose cinnamon, frankincense, lily of the valley, angelica, bayberry, jasmine, pine, patchouli, club moss, dill, fern, dragon's blood, juniper, hazel, hawthorn, fir, feverfew, pepper, marjoram, oak, thistle, or furze.

14

A FEW MAGIC SPELLS

You can consider this chapter as a bonus chapter. I wanted to give you something that will help you get started on your magical journey, so I decided to include a few magic spells.

Before you dive into your spellwork, I want to reiterate the most important facts from this book: the need to thoroughly understand Celtic magic, how to cast a circle, what tools to use, and how to make sure that you are confident in your next steps. If you feel that you could use a refresher on how to prepare for your spellwork or how to cast a circle correctly, then take a look at Chapter 2 or Chapter 4 before you begin. You also want to look to see how prepared you are for this chapter. For example, have you set up your altar? What magical tools do you have? You need to know this so you know what spell you can start with and which ones you should wait for, at least until you are prepared.

The spells covered in this chapter will include some with candles, herbs, and other tools. I tried to find easy spells for beginners that will work with some of the most straightforward tools available.

Herbs

One of the first spells people should learn is how to remove negativity from their homes. No matter how much you try, it is impossible not to let negativity seep into your home. Part of this is because of the world we live in, one where so many people belittle each other and try to harm one another for various reasons. If you are watching the local news and hear about a brutal murder in your area, you can allow negativity into your home by listening to the story and feeling dislike toward the suspect or sorrow about the story. Negativity tends to squeeze into your life when you are unaware, and it can stay there until you notice it and try to cast it out, or you perform a regular cleansing or spell.

Banishing Negativity

One of the easiest spells to banish negativity from the home uses basil. It is basically an in-depth cleansing. First, you need to cast a circle of protection around yourself. You will move around your home, so you do not need to use your altar for this spell. Next, you will add basil to each corner within your home. You only want to sprinkle a little on the floors. You will want to make sure you get every corner in every room. You will then run a bath and sprinkle basil into your bathwater. One of the best ways to release the negativity is to say a prayer and ask for your higher powers to help you. You might call on certain gods or goddesses that focus on banishing negativity. Some people will simply take a bath after sprinkling basil around the home and then visualize all the negativity removing itself through the windows and the doorway.

Trouble with Insomnia

Do you have trouble sleeping? If you do, there is a spell you can perform with chamomile, sometimes called ground apple, wild chamomile, or roman chamomile. All you need to do is add two teaspoons of the herb into a cup of water and boil it for about five minutes. Drink the tea, and you will notice it gently puts you to sleep.

Creating Protection

Once you start getting more involved with your magic, you will come across moments where you need to cast a circle of protection quickly when you are outside. This can happen when you feel a negative entity near you or for another reason. As long as you can find a hazel branch, you can quickly draw a circle of protection around yourself. You do not need to stay in one spot as you can move around with the circle. The key is to try to bring some hazelnuts home with you as you can make a string of hazelnuts and hang it up in your home. Doing this will call on the plant fairies, who will make sure that you are taken care of, and nothing negative will harm you.

Peace in the Home

We all want to add a little peace into our home. We can do this by burning candles that give off peaceful energy or finding the purple loosestrife herb and placing it in each corner of your home. You will want to make sure you walk along with every room, so you get every corner. This includes attics and basements. If you have an attached garage, you also want to sprinkle the purple loosestrife in the garage. From there, you simply go about your day and allow the herb to do its magic.

Producing Clairvoyant Dreams

If you want to increase your clairvoyant dreams, remember them, or understand them better, then you want to purchase marigold. All you need to do is add some of the herbs underneath your pillow. It will help you with your dreams. You can also use a liquid marigold to help you see fairies by rubbing it on your eyelids.

Luck and Money

Asking for an increase in money and luck is another common spell among people. Once you start getting into your spellwork, you will learn that a lot of spells focus on increasing your wealth and good luck. One of the easiest good luck spells that can also give you a little more money is used with the herb known as Irish moss, sometimes called pearl moss. Known for keeping a steady stream of money coming your way, all you need to do is burn the herb with incense while you recite a spell for good luck or money. Once the herb is cooled, sprinkle a little of it inside of your billfold or purse for added good luck.

Protection Against Dark Magic

Rue is another herb that is a defense against negativity, but more specifically, dark magic. This type of magic can happen accidentally when someone does not understand what they are doing and tries to perform a good spell that turns bad. To protect yourself from this type of magic, whether on purpose or accident, you want to sprinkle the water of the rue, which can be found in a sprig form. If you can't find rue in a sprig form, you can use the herb in another way and burn it with purification incense. It will help move the negativity away from you and your home.

Using Your Cauldron

Before you begin using your cauldron, you need to understand the importance of timing when it comes to your magic. Sometimes the best time is during a full moon while other spells are best performed after a full moon. Some are stronger at night while others work best during the day. Timing is something that you might feel in your gut, or you might find yourself reading about the best time to perform a specific spell in the spell's directions. You will also learn when the most suitable time to work your magic is. The trick is to keep your mind open.

If you are looking for love, you want to place your cauldron between two pink candles on your altar. If not, everything will sit well on your altar (always remember safety when it comes to candles and fire), then you can perform this spell near your altar. Set a magenta candle onto your altar and light a love incense and then the two pink candles. With your wand, gently tap the side of your cauldron three times and say the following or similar words:

"I am seeking him/her. I wish to find him/her. Please help me, dear one, by bringing him/her to me. Bind him/her to me. Our hearts together forever. So I say, and this spell is done."

Then you will gently tap the side of the cauldron three more times and light the magenta candle. The best time to perform this spell is during the waxing moon, preferably around midnight.

Growing Your Wealth

To increase your wealth, you want to fill your cauldron with water up to the half-way mark. Drop a silver coin into the cauldron, which you will set in a certain way to allow the light from the moon to shine on the water. Sweep your hands above the surface gently as this is a symbolic way to gather the silver from the moon. While you are sweeping your hand, you want to repeat the following or similar words:

"My dear lovely lady in the moon, please send your wealth soon. My hands are open to you so you can fill them with gold and silver. Fill my purse with all you can give."

You will repeat these words three times and then take your cauldron and pour the water on the ground. The best time to perform this spell is during a full moon.

Things to Remember:

One of the biggest factors to remember about spells is that they are not concrete. While you want to make sure that your circle of protection is closed and negativity cannot get out, you want to use your magical tools wisely, and ensure that you pick candles and incense that match the spell. You can simply make up your own spells or change the wording. All you need to do is look back to Chapter 13 and see what candles and incense are required to perform a love or good luck spell. Once you have the supplies, you can set it up like a regular spell, such as wearing your cloak and setting out your directional candles and then following your instincts. Always remember your instincts are your most reliable guides.

CONCLUSION

By now, you have a good idea about Celtic history, tradition, and how to cast a few easy spells. You understand that each color on the candle has meaning and that some incense will work better with some spells than others. You also know that you always need to think of safety and make sure that you close your circle of protection and do not step out of the circle as you are performing the spell.

Remember, it is more important to go slow and steady when you are learning about magic than to try to speed your learning along. While it happens, making a mistake when you are casting your circle or spell can cause the spell not to work, or worse, invites negative thoughts or energies into your circle, home, or your body.

Do not allow your learning to stop with this book. While it is a comprehensive book when it comes to Celtic magic and the Druids, you never want to stop learning. There are centuries of information that you can read about the Druids because they still exist today. They are still some of the most spiritual people that pray for peace in this world you would ever meet.

REFERENCES

Ancient Pages. (2019). Lugh - Mighty god of light, sun and crafts in Celtic beliefs. Retrieved 7 January 2020, from http://www.ancientpages.com/2018/04/30/lugh-mighty-god-of-light-sun-and-crafts-in-celtic-beliefs/

Angel Fire. (n.d.). Introduction to the Celtic Religion. https://docs.google.com/document/d/1VaSFJvK8PQQy3yb-RDZpT1mo1BCQKOVHxRNAaPLY58e0/edit#

Bisdent. (2012). Epona. In Ancient History Encyclopedia. Retrieved 3 January 2020, from https://www.ancient.eu/article/153/epona/

Blank, B. (n.d.) Taranis: The thunderer. Druidry. https://www.druidry.org/library/gods-goddesses/taranis-thunderer

Celtic Life. (2017). CELTIC GODS & GODDESSES. https://celticlife.com/celtic-gods-goddesses/

Celts and Myths. (2014). Belenus - Belenos - a sun god in Celtic mythology. http://celtsandmyths.mzzhost.com/belenus.html

Conway, D. (2012). Celtic Magic, p.22. Books.google.com. Excerpt retrieved 10 January 2020, from https://books.google.com/books?id=b9WTSC1maywC&ppis=_e&lpg=PA13&ots=6JZGn7biHi&dq=preparing%20for%20magic%20Celtic&pg=PA22#v=onepage&q=preparing%20for%20magic%20Celtic&f=false

Druidry. (n.d.a). Sacred sites. https://www.druidry.org/library/sacred-sites

Druidry. (n.d.b). What is a Druid? https://www.druidry.org/druid-way/what-druidry/what-druidism/what-druid

Druidry. (n.d.c). Wicca & Druidcraft. https://www.druidry.org/druid-way/other-paths/wicca-druidcraft

Greer, J. (2016). The Druid magic handbook. Issuu. https://issuu.com/soulshine.tonya/docs/john_michael_greer_-_the_-druid_magi

Gruben, M. (2017). Circle-casting basics: All you need to know about magick circles. Grove and Grotto. Retrieved 4 January 2020, from https://www.groveandgrotto.com/blogs/articles/circle-casting-basics-all-you-need-to-know-about-magick-circles

Hughes, K. (2014). The book of Celtic magic. Issuu. https://issuu.com/llewellyn/docs/9780738737058/18

Ireland-Information.com (n.d.). Irish myths & legends: The Tuatha de Danann - Ireland's greatest tribe. http://www.ireland-information.com/irish-mythology/tuatha-de-danann-irish-legend.html

Isaac, A. (2016). The Tuatha De Danann: Were they Irish gods or aliens? (PHOTOS). IrishCentral.com. https://www.irishcentral.com/roots/ancestry/the-tuatha-de-danann-were-they-irish-gods-or-aliens-photos

Louv, J. (2018). Tapping in to the four elements. Blog.magick.me. Retrieved 9 January 2020, from https://blog.magick.me/2018/01/25/four-elements/

Magic Love Spells. (2019). How to prepare for a ritual or spell. Retrieved 3 January 2020, from https://www.magic-love-spells.com/how-to-prepare-for-a-ritual-or-spell/

McCoy, E. (1995). Celtic myth & magick: Harness the power of the gods & goddesses. St. Paul, MN: Llewellyn Publications. https://books.google.com/books?

id=igtmLDLpF7YC&pg=PT113&lpg=PT113&dq=the+esbats+Celts&source=bl&ots=rPVVXij1VS&sig=

ACfU3U0KeGFiU_8uzbY4GoNIQdu9rm-Sy3Q&hl=en&ppis=_e&sa=X&ved=2ahUKEwjl8_ODvojnAhWHKM0KHeafA2MQ6AEwD30ECAsQAQ#v=

onepage&q=the%20esbats%20Celts&f=false

Melia, C. (1999). Animals and birds in Celtic tradition. Celtic Heritage. http://www.celticheritage.co.uk/articles_animals.cfm

Murphy, A. (2019). Ancient sites | The Lia Fáil - mystery screeching stone of Tara brought by the Tuatha Dé Danann. Mythical Ireland. Retrieved 14 January 2020, from https://www.mythicalireland.com/ancient-sites/the-lia-fail-mystery-screeching-stone-of-tara-brought-by-the-tuatha-de-danann/

Sacred Fire. (n.d.). Rituals & Charms. https://www.sacredfire.net/ritual.html

Sullivan, K. (2019). Tuatha Dé Dannan, the enchanting predecessors of Irish fairies and elves. Ancient-Origins.

https://www.ancient-origins.net/myths-legends/tuatha-d-dannan-enchanting-predecessors-irish-fairies-and-elves-007657

The Celtic Journey. (2013a). Faeries. https://thecelticjourney.wordpress.com/2013/04/21/faeries/

The Celtic Journey. (2013b). Nuada of the silver arm. https://thecelticjourney.wordpress.com/tag/nuada/

The Celtic Witch. (n.d.) Casting a Circle. https://thecelticwitch.net/casting-a-circle

The White Goddess. (n.d.). Tuireann - God of thunder. - Irish god. http://www.thewhitegoddess.co.uk/divinity_of_the_day/irish/tuireann.asp

Wicca. (n.d.) Celtic Deities. https://wicca.com/celtic/wicca/celtic.htm

Wigington, P. (2018a). Brighid, the hearth goddess of Ireland. Learn Religions. Retrieved 3 January 2020, from https://www.learnreligions.com/brighid-hearth-goddess-of-ireland-2561958

Wigington, P. (2018b). Cailleach, the ruler of winter. Learn Religions. Retrieved 3 January 2020, from https://www.learnreligions.com/cailleach-the-ruler-of-winter-2561705

Wigington, P. (2018c). Setting up your magical altar. Learn Religions. Retrieved 3 January 2020, from https://www.learnreligions.com/setting-up-your-magical-altar-2561940

Wigington, P. (2019). Rhiannon, horse goddess of Wales. Learn Religions. Retrieved 3 January 2020, from https://www.learnreligions.com/rhiannon-horse-goddess-of-wales-2561707

World Spirituality. (n.d.) Celtic Otherworld. http://www.worldspirituality.org/celtic-otherworld.html

ABOUT THE AUTHOR

Monique Joiner Siedlak: Author, Witch, Warrior.

With storytelling infused with mysticism, modern paganism, and new age spirituality, Monique awakens your potential. Initiated into the craft at 20, her 80+ books explore the magick and mysteries of life.

A Long Island native, she now calls Southeast Poland home but remains a citizen of Mother Earth.

Beyond her pen, Monique craves new experiences and cherishes nature, advocating for animal welfare.

Join her captivating journey as she transports you to enchanting realms and empowers your own transformative path. Unleash the dormant magic within and embrace the extraordinary with Monique Joiner Siedlak's evocative words.

To find out more about Monique artistically, spiritually, and personally, feel free to visit her **official website.**

www.mojcsiedlak.com

facebook.com/mojosiedlak

x.com/mojosiedlak

instagram.com/mojosiedlak

youtube.com/@MoniqueJoinerSiedlak_Author

tiktok.com/@mojosiedlak

bookbub.com/authors/monique-joiner-siedlak

pinterest.com/mojosiedlak

African Spirituality Beliefs and Practices

Hoodoo

Seven African Powers: The Orishas

Cooking for the Orishas

Lucumi: The Ways of Santeria

Voodoo of Louisiana

Haitian Vodou

Orishas of Trinidad

Connecting with your Ancestors

Blood Magick

The Orishas

Vodun: West Africa's Spiritual Life

Marie Laveau: Life of a Voodoo Queen

Candomblé: Dancing for the God

Umbanda

Exploring the Rich and Diverse World

Divination Magic for Beginners

Divination with Runes

Divination with Diloggún

Divination with Osteomancy

Divination with the Tarot

Divination with Stones

The Beginner's Guide to Inner Growth

Astral Projection for Beginners

Meditation for Beginners

Reiki for Beginners

Mastering Your Inner Potential

Creative Visualization

Manifesting With the Law of Attraction

Holistic Healing and Energy

Healing Animals with Reiki

Crystal Healing

Communicating with Your Spirit Guides

Empathic Understanding and Enlightenment

Being an Empath Today

Life on Fire

Healing Your Inner Child

Change Your Life

Raising Your Vibe

The Indie Author's Guides

The Indie Author's Guide to Fast Drafting Your Novel

Get a Handle on Life

Get a Handle on Stress

Time Bound

Get a Handle on Anxiety

Get a Handle on Depression

Get a Handle on Procrastination

The Holistic Yoga and Wellness Series

Yoga for Beginners

Yoga for Stress

Yoga for Back Pain

Yoga for Weight Loss

Yoga for Flexibility

Yoga for Advanced Beginners

Yoga for Fitness

Yoga for Runners

Yoga for Energy

Yoga for Your Sex Life

Yoga to Beat Depression and Anxiety

Yoga for Menstruation

Yoga to Detox Your Body

Yoga to Tone Your Body

The DIY Body Care Series

Creating Your Own Body Butter

Creating Your Own Body Scrub

Creating Your Own Body Spray

SUPPORT ME BY LEAVING A REVIEW!

⭐ ⭐ ⭐ ⭐ ⭐

goodreads

www.ingramcontent.com/pod-product-compliance
Lightning Source LLC
Chambersburg PA
CBHW060838050426
42453CB00008B/745